P9-DYP-506

R02084 70976

DATE DUE

CHRISTIANITY

Russian
Orthodox
icons

Salvation
Army
song
leader
playing a
cornet

Abbot's
crozier

Holy
water
stoup

Horn of Saint
Hubert

Stained glass fragment
depicting the Madonna
and Child

Model of
the *Mayflower*

DK EYEWITNESS BOOKS

CHRISTIANITY

Written by
PHILIP WILKINSON

Photographed by
STEVE TEAGUE

Illuminated Latin psalter

DK Publishing

Carving of
an angel
swinging
a censer

Gargoyle

Censer and
incense
boat on
stand

Statue of
Saint Joseph

DK

LONDON, NEW YORK, MUNICH,
MELBOURNE, and DELHI

For Bookwork Ltd:
Editor Annabel Blackledge
Art editor Kate Mullins

For Dorling Kindersley Ltd:
Managing editor Andrew Macintyre
Managing art editors
Clare Shedden, Jane Thomas
US editors
Margaret Parrish, Christine Heilman
Category publisher Linda Martin
Production controller Erica Rosen
Picture researchers
Angela Anderson, Bridget Tily
Picture librarian Claire Bowers
DTP designer Siu Yin Ho
Jacket Designer Dean Price

Consultants
Annette Reynolds, AD Publishing Services Ltd,
Jon Reynolds, Diocesan Director of Education

First American Edition, 2003
03 04 05 06 07 10 9 8 7 6 5 4 3 2 1

Published in the United States by
DK Publishing, Inc.
375 Hudson Street
New York, New York 10014

A Cataloging-in-Publication
record for this book is available from
the Library of Congress

ISBN 0-7894-9239-3

Color reproduction by
Colourscan, Singapore
Printed in Hong Kong
by Toppan

See our complete
product line at
www.dk.com

Bread and wine for
Holy Communion

Rosary
with medals

Rosary
medal

Model of a
baroque
church

Contents

Abbot in ceremonial robes

In the beginning

THE BIBLE BEGINS WITH stories of the creation of the world and the early Jewish people. These books, which make up the Old Testament of the Christian Bible, and which are also sacred to the Jews, were written by Jewish scribes long before the birth of Jesus. For the Jews they are important because they describe the covenant, or special relationship, between God and the Jewish people. For Christians the Old Testament has added significance because many of the stories seem to prefigure, or mirror, events that happened later when Jesus came to save humankind from sin.

Fourth-century depiction of Adam and Eve in Eden

FORBIDDEN FRUIT
Genesis, the first book of the Bible (p. 20), tells how God created Heaven and Earth, land and water, animals and birds, and finally Adam and Eve—the first man and woman. God put them in the Garden of Eden, and told them that the only fruit they must not eat was the fruit of the Tree of Knowledge.

ENEMY IN EDEN
Satan, who lived in Hell (pp. 26–27), was God's archenemy. Early Jewish writers said that the serpent in the Garden of Eden, a cunning tempter, was Satan in disguise. In the Book of Genesis, the serpent tempts Eve to eat the forbidden fruit, just as Satan later tempted Jesus in the New Testament.

The serpent is often pictured as a snake like this red spitting cobra

Satan

This 12th-century painting of Satan shows him with Saint Michael

Saint Michael is weighing souls to determine whether they should go to Heaven or Hell

The forbidden fruit is often imagined to have been an apple

ORIGINAL SIN
The serpent tempted Eve to eat the forbidden fruit, and Adam followed suit. God was angry at their disobedience and threw them out of the Garden of Eden. Christians believe that Adam and Eve, and their descendants, were tainted with this "original sin." Only the coming of Jesus Christ would eventually offer humankind a way of escaping sin and achieving everlasting life with God.

The dove brought Noah a leaf to show that the flood waters were going down

Mosaic of Noah and his family in the ark

THE GREAT FLOOD

Another story in Genesis tells how God became disenchanted with all the evil in the world, and sent a great flood to destroy much of the wickedness. Only one good man, Noah, was allowed to escape with his family. He built a great boat, the ark, in which he, his sons and their wives, and all the birds and animals took refuge. Christians think of Noah as the second father of the human race, after Adam.

> *"Do not lay a hand on the boy, he said. Do not do anything to him. Now I know that you fear God."*

GENESIS 22:12
Angel of the Lord to Abraham

God provided a ram for Abraham's sacrifice

SACRIFICIAL RAM

God ordered Abraham to kill his son Isaac as a sacrifice. Abraham was about to obey when an angel told him to stop and kill a ram instead. Christians see this story as a prophecy of the way in which God would sacrifice Jesus.

Daniel window from Augsburg Cathedral in Germany

Isaiah window from Augsburg Cathedral in Germany

Moses window from Augsburg Cathedral in Germany

PROPHETS AND LEADERS

The Old Testament contains stories about Jewish ancestors such as Abraham and the great leader Moses, who guided the Jews from slavery in Egypt back to their homeland. The Old Testament also includes writings about and by prophets such as Isaiah and Daniel, who told of the coming of a Messiah, or savior.

The birth of Jesus

HUMBLE BEGINNINGS
Mary and Joseph were staying in Bethlehem at the time of the nativity, or birth, of Jesus. All the inns in the town were full, so Jesus had to be born in the humblest of surroundings—a stable.

THE GOSPELS (p. 21) tell how a virgin called Mary gave birth to Jesus Christ in Bethlehem. Followers of Christ (Christians) believe that Jesus was God's son, and that the prophets of the Old Testament had predicted he would come and save humankind from sin. The idea that God became human in this way is called the incarnation, meaning that God's spirit was made into human flesh. The birth of Jesus marked the origin of the Christian religion.

The angels play instruments that were popular in the 16th century, when this altarpiece was made

Mary is traditionally shown wearing blue

MADONNA AND CHILD
Statues of Mary, or the Madonna, and the infant Jesus are a reminder of Mary's vital role in the Christian story. She is a link between the human and spiritual worlds.

The Holy Spirit is shown in the form of a dove

Modern mosaic from Old Plaza Church in California

THE ANNUNCIATION
Luke's Gospel describes how the angel Gabriel appeared to Mary to tell her that, even though she was a virgin, she was about to become pregnant. Gabriel announced that Mary would be visited by the Holy Spirit (p. 26) and would give birth to God's son, who would be a king whose rule would last forever. Mary was told to call her son Jesus.

John carries a banner bearing Latin words meaning "Behold the Lamb of God"

John wears camel-hair clothes, the typical garments of a prophet

JOHN THE BAPTIST
John led the life of a prophet and preacher, encouraging people to repent their sins and be baptized. John's preaching prepared the way for Jesus, and when Jesus grew up he asked John to baptize him in the Jordan River.

Statue by Donatello, 1386–1466

GLAD TIDINGS
Luke's account of the nativity describes how angels appeared to shepherds in the fields just outside Bethlehem. The angels told them the good news of Jesus' birth and the shepherds came down from the fields into the town to worship the newborn king. This story shows that Jesus is important to everyone, even "outsiders" like the shepherds.

God looks down from Heaven

FOLLOW THE STAR
Matthew's Gospel tells how the Magi, or wise men, followed a star from the east to Jerusalem in search of a child born to rule the people of Israel. King Herod sent them to Bethlehem, where they found Jesus.

14th-century pendant showing the Magi and Jesus

Gold

Frankincense

Myrrh

FIT FOR A KING
The Magi worshipped Jesus and gave him three gifts: gold, frankincense, and myrrh. The symbolism of these gifts may be interpreted in different ways. One interpretation is that gold represents riches, frankincense kingship, and myrrh a special spiritual calling.

The shepherds watch their flocks of sheep

15th-century stained glass from Ulm Cathedral in Germany

ROYAL RIVALRY
King Herod ruled the Holy Land on behalf of the Romans. According to Matthew, he tried to destroy Jesus, whom he saw as a rival to his throne. Herod told his men to kill all the children in Bethlehem who were less than two years old. God warned Joseph of this, and he escaped with Mary and Jesus to Egypt.

Mary, her husband Joseph, and the baby Jesus

Glazed earthenware altarpiece made by Giovanni della Robbia, 1521

The teachings of Jesus

J ESUS' MINISTRY—his period of teaching—probably lasted no more than three years, but it had an enormous impact. During this short time he preached, taught, and performed miracles in the Holy Land, especially in the villages around the Sea of Galilee. Jesus was a brilliant teacher who could explain things in ways that everyone could understand. His teachings attracted many followers because they revealed a new way of looking at God's kingdom. He said it was open to all believers who would turn away from their sins, including the poor, the sick, and social outcasts.

FISHERS OF MEN
As this Italian mosaic shows, Andrew and Simon were fishermen. Jesus called them to be his disciples, telling them that, if they followed him, he would teach them to catch people (enlist new followers of Christ) instead of fish.

GOD'S OWN SON
The Gospels describe how, when Jesus was baptized (p. 58), the Holy Spirit came down like a dove and God's voice was heard saying, "This is my own dear Son." This momentous event, shown here in a fifth-century mosaic from Ravenna, Italy, marks the beginning of Jesus' ministry.

A LIFE IN GLASS
This window from St. Albans Cathedral in Hertfordshire, England, shows key episodes from the life of Jesus. It includes his baptism, the water into wine miracle, and the Crucifixion. The bottom right-hand panel of the window shows Jesus as a shepherd, a symbol of the way in which he cared for the people around him.

Jesus on the cross surrounded by Roman soldiers and the two Marys

Jesus turns water into wine at Cana

HUMBLE LEADER
Jesus called 12 disciples to be his special companions. They were expected to leave their families and possessions to follow and help Jesus, and carry on his work after his death. When he washed the disciples' feet, as shown on this French manuscript, Jesus was showing them that they should be as humble as their leader.

Terra-cotta jars
for storing water

Continued on next page

FEEDING THE MULTITUDE

This is the only miracle described in all four of the Gospels. After a long day's preaching, Jesus and the disciples wished to rest, but they were followed by a vast crowd who wanted to hear Jesus speak. Jesus felt sorry that the crowd had no food, and produced enough for all of them from the only available foodstuffs—five small loaves and two fishes.

The miracles

The Gospels describe more than 30 of Jesus' miracles. Some of these involved feeding the needy, others were "nature miracles," such as calming the storm or walking on the water. But the majority involved some sort of healing— either curing people of physical diseases like leprosy and paralysis or "casting out demons" to rid people of mental illness. The Gospels record three occasions when Jesus even raised people from the dead.

WATER INTO WINE

Jesus' first miracle, which is described in John's Gospel, took place at a wedding that he attended at Cana in Galilee. When the wine ran out, Jesus told the servants to fill six large pots with water, and when they poured the liquid out of the pots it had turned into wine. The wine was so good that the guests thought the bridegroom had kept the best until last.

TAX COLLECTORS

Some members of a Jewish group called the Pharisees tried to trick Jesus into criticizing the Roman authorities. They asked him whether it was right that they should pay taxes to the Romans. Jesus showed them the emperor's portrait on the coins and said that they should give the emperor what belonged to him.

Paying the tax collector

CALMING WATERS

Jesus grew up in Nazareth, but moved to Capernaum, on the banks of the Sea of Galilee, where he began his ministry. Jesus did much of his teaching in this region, and one of his miracles was the calming of a storm on the lake's waters. When he wanted a quiet place to pray, Jesus traveled into the local hills, which can be seen in the background of this photograph of the Sea of Galilee's northern shore.

Parables and lessons

Jesus' favorite way of teaching was to use parables— short stories that make their point by means of a simple comparison. Jesus used these parables to talk about the kingdom of God, and to illustrate how people should behave toward each other. Jesus also preached moral lectures called sermons. The most famous of these was the Sermon on the Mount, in which he explained the key features of the kingdom of God (p. 26) and the Christian way of life. Above all, Jesus said that you should "Do for others what you want them to do for you."

THE LOST SON
This parable tells of a man who divided his wealth between his two sons. The younger son went off and spent his share, while his brother worked hard at home. When the younger son returned, his father killed his prize calf for a celebratory feast. The elder son objected, but his father said, "He was lost, but now he has been found." These Chinese illustrations show the story from the handing over of the money to the family feast.

SERMON ON THE MOUNT
In this sermon Jesus said that members of God's kingdom should try to achieve the perfection shown by God. For example, he explained that it is not enough simply to obey the commandment, "Do not commit murder." Christians should avoid anger completely.

The disciples have haloes, to indicate their holiness

19th-century window of the Good Samaritan

THE GOOD SAMARITAN
Jesus taught that you should love your neighbor. When someone asked Jesus, "Who is my neighbor?" he told this story: A man was robbed and left for dead. A Jewish priest and a Levite passed, but did not help. Then a Samaritan—a member of a group scorned by the Jews—came by. He helped the injured man and took him to safety. The Samaritan was the true neighbor.

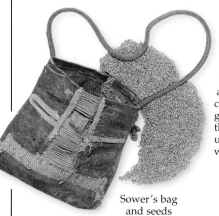

PLANTING WORDS
Jesus compared his words to seeds scattered by a farmer. Some of the seed fell on the path and was stepped on. Some fell on rocky ground or among thorn bushes, where seedlings could not grow. Finally, some fell on good soil and grew into corn. Jesus said that people who heard and understood his words were like the good soil.

Sower's bag and seeds

Figs and fig leaf

LESSON OF THE FIG TREE
Jesus told people to think of a fig tree. When its leaves start to appear, people know that summer is on its way. Similarly, they should look out for signs of Jesus' second coming. When strange things happen to the moon and stars, when whole countries are in despair, and people are faint from fear, then they will know that the kingdom of God is about to come.

Jesus would probably have sat down to deliver the sermon

THE LORD'S PRAYER

Jesus gave his most important lesson about prayer in the Sermon on the Mount. He told his listeners not to pray ostentatiously with long, elaborate prayers—God knows what you need before you ask. Instead, he gave them the *Lord's Prayer* beginning, "Our Father in Heaven, hallowed be your name…". It has been translated into languages as diverse as Spanish and Chinese, and is repeated in Christian churches the world over.

Horn book with the text of the *Lord's Prayer* in Latin

15th-century fresco by Fra Angelico

"Blessed are the merciful, for they will be shown mercy. Blessed are the pure in heart, for they will see God."

MATTHEW 5:7–8
Jesus' Sermon on the Mount

Common poppies

FLOWERY FINERY

During the Sermon on the Mount, Jesus told his listeners that they should not care too much about everyday things like food and clothes. Wild flowers do not have fine garments, but they are still beautifully dressed. People should be concerned with God's kingdom, not with possessions or finery.

The Crucifixion

JESUS WARNED HIS DISCIPLES several times that he would soon die. He told them that the Jewish chief priests would reject him, that he would be killed, and that he would rise again after three days. The disciples failed to understand these warnings, and were unprepared for what happened when Jesus went to Jerusalem. Jesus was put on trial and condemned to death on the cross. This is the most solemn part of the Christian story, but it is also the major turning point—Christians believe Jesus' blood was spilled so that they could be granted eternal life with God.

ON THE CROSS
In Jesus' time crucifixion was the normal way in which the Romans imposed the death sentence. Jesus was crucified between two criminals, and the Gospels recall that his death took about three hours—much faster than usual. At the point of Jesus' death the curtain in the Temple in Jerusalem was torn in two and an earthquake shook the ground.

Christ looks triumphant, not suffering

10th-century crucifix from Denmark, made of gilded carved oak

Rosary medal showing Jesus carrying his cross

BODY AND BLOOD
At the Last Supper with his disciples, Jesus broke the bread and told them to eat it, saying, "This is my body." He then gave them the wine, saying, "This is my blood." When Christians celebrate Communion (pp. 52–53) they remember or recreate these events.

ENTRY INTO JERUSALEM
Jesus rode into Jerusalem on a donkey, as shown in this painting from the Oratory of Saint Pellegrino in Italy. Many people laid down palm leaves, or even their coats, to cover the dusty path in front of him. They were happy because the prophet Zechariah had predicted that their king would arrive on a donkey.

Jesus is shown with the marks of the nails in his palms

14

THE ROAD TO CALVARY
Jesus was flogged and mocked before his death. Because he had been called King of the Jews he was forced to wear a crown of thorns. He was made to carry his heavy cross along the steep road to Calvary, the place of crucifixion. Jesus tried but he was too weak, so a spectator, Simon of Cyrene, carried it for him.

Rosary medal showing Jesus wearing the crown of thorns

A CONDEMNED MAN
The council elders took Jesus to Pontius Pilate, the Roman governor, who had the power to impose the death penalty. Jesus was accused of setting himself up as King of the Jews but, when asked about this, Jesus simply said, "So you say." Pilate was unwilling to condemn Jesus, and said the crowd could choose one prisoner to be set free. But they refused to release Jesus.

IN DENIAL
Jesus was taken to the High Priest, Caiaphas, and was put before the supreme Jewish council. As the disciple Peter sat outside he was accused three times of being one of Jesus' followers, but he denied it each time. A rooster crowed as Peter made his third denial. Jesus had told Peter that this would happen.

Many churches have a rooster weather vane to remind us of the denial

13th-century Syriac manuscript

THE LAST SUPPER
At the time of Jesus' arrest it was Passover—the festival that celebrates the freeing of the Jews from slavery and looks forward to the coming of the Messiah. Jesus told his disciples to arrange a Passover meal. He said that this would be the last meal he would share with them and that one of them would soon betray him.

The Kiss of Judas by Giotto di Bondone

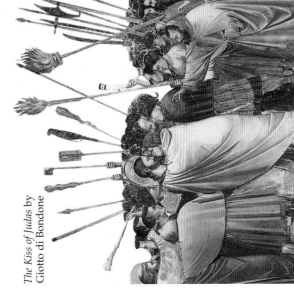

JUDAS KISS
After the Last Supper, Jesus went to the Garden of Gethsemane. His disciple Judas Iscariot arrived with Roman soldiers and the Jewish Temple guard. Judas greeted Jesus with a kiss—a signal he had arranged with the soldiers. The soldiers arrested Jesus, who told his disciples not to resist but to accept God's will.

The Resurrection

(p. 21)

CHRISTIANS BELIEVE that on the third day after his crucifixion Jesus rose from the dead. The Gospels (p. 21) describe how, when he appeared to his disciples after the Resurrection, some of them did not recognize him. Jesus' body seemed to have changed, and he apparently was able to appear and disappear at will. Christians believe in the Resurrection in different ways. Some are convinced that the risen Jesus was literally alive on Earth. Others believe his presence was a spiritual one, seen only in the ways in which his followers behaved. Most Christians believe that Jesus joined God in Heaven, where he will stay until the Last Judgment (p. 26).

STRONG SYMBOL
The Resurrection is one of the most important parts of the Christian story. It is often depicted symbolically, as in the case of this embroidered decoration from a priest's clothing.

John, whose symbol is an eagle

Matthew, whose symbol is a man

THE EMPTY CROSS
An empty cross is a reminder of Jesus' resurrection. The lamb at the center is a familiar symbol of Jesus, who is often referred to as the Lamb of God. The lamb is an innocent creature that is easily killed, so it reminds Christians of the sacrifice made by God in order to redeem humankind from sin.

ROCK TOMB
Joseph of Arimathea, a disciple of Jesus, offered his own tomb for Jesus' burial. This tomb was probably similar to the one above. Called an arcosolium, it has been cut into the rock of a cliff face and sealed with a large, round stone.

Mark, whose symbol is a lion

RISEN FROM THE DEAD
Pontius Pilate ordered soldiers to guard Jesus' tomb in case the disciples came to take away his body. But the Gospels tell how, on the third day after the Crucifixion, Jesus rose from the dead while the guards slept. This set of three 15th-century Italian paintings (see also opposite) shows Jesus rising from a Roman-style sarcophagus, or tomb, set into the rocks.

SUPPER AT EMMAUS
Shortly after the Resurrection, Jesus met two of his disciples near a village called Emmaus. The pair did not recognize him, but invited him to supper with some other disciples. It was only when Jesus broke the bread and blessed it that they recognized him. Then he disappeared from their sight.

Illustration from a 15th-century Italian Bible

DOUBTING THOMAS
The disciple Thomas said that he would believe in Jesus' resurrection only if he saw the wounds that Jesus had received when he was crucified. John's Gospel recalls that, when Jesus met the disciples, he showed Thomas his wounds.

Mural from the Holy Trinity Church in Sopocani, Serbia, c. 1265

Jesus is shown surrounded by clouds and angels

THE ASCENSION
The Gospels and another New Testament book called Acts record that, after telling his disciples to spread the word (pp. 18–19), Jesus joined his Father in Heaven. He was raised up into the sky and then vanished behind a cloud.

12th-century stone relief from Saint Dominic's Abbey in Silos, Spain

> *"The Christ will suffer and rise from the dead on the third day."*
>
> **LUKE 24:46**
> Jesus to his disciples

Luke, whose symbol is an ox

THE EMPTY TOMB
A group of women, probably including Jesus' follower Mary Magdalene, went to the tomb to anoint his body with spices. When they arrived, they found the tomb open and empty. An angel appeared to them and told them that Jesus had risen from the dead. In Matthew's account of this story, the amazing news was accompanied by an earthquake.

LOOKING FOR JESUS
John's Gospel contains a moving account of Mary Magdalene's search for Jesus' body. As she wept at his disappearance, a man appeared whom Mary believed to be a gardener. But when he spoke her name, she realized immediately that it was Jesus. He said, "Do not hold on to me, because I have not yet gone back up to the Father."

Spreading the word

IN THE DECADES following Jesus' crucifixion, his disciples continued his work of teaching and preaching. Saint Paul was the most important of these early preachers. He founded churches around the Mediterranean, and his letters to these and other churches make up many of the books of the New Testament. These letters have proved a source of inspiration to the countless others who have come after Paul and who have worked to spread Christianity around the world.

TONGUES LIKE FIRE
The Book of Acts describes how the disciples were gathered together for an ancient Jewish festival called Pentecost. There was a sound like a wind blowing through the room, and tongues like fire spread out and touched each disciple, filling them with the Holy Spirit. Pentecost took on a new significance to Christians after this day.

The seated disciples are surrounded by tongues like flame

Catacombs of Priscalla, Rome, Italy

PASSIONATE SAINT PETER
Peter, as pictured on this 1430s Italian prayer book, was one of the leaders of the disciples. At Pentecost, he spoke passionately to the others, telling them that they had been visited by the Holy Spirit and saying that Jesus had risen from the dead and was the Messiah promised by God.

PERSECUTED CHRISTIANS
After Pentecost, the Christian community started to grow, and Peter began to allow non-Jews to join the church. The Roman authorities did not approve of Christianity, however, and many believers were persecuted. When the faith spread to Rome itself, many Christians kept their beliefs secret, even going down into the catacombs (underground tombs) to worship.

Saint Paul

Saul was a Roman citizen and a Jew. He persecuted Christians and was present at the death of Stephen, the first Christian martyr (someone who dies for their faith). While on a journey to Damascus in Syria, Saul was temporarily blinded by a dazzling light, and he heard the voice of God asking him why he was attacking the church.

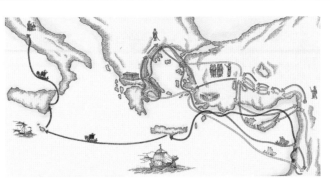

PAUL'S JOURNEYS
After his vision on the road to Damascus, Saul converted to Christianity and took the name Paul. He traveled around the Mediterranean, converting people to Christianity and setting up churches. As shown by this map, Paul's journeys took him to Cyprus, Turkey, Macedonia, and Greece.

ANCIENT EPHESUS
The ancient city of Ephesus (now in Turkey) was the site of one of the most important churches founded by Paul. His letter to the Ephesians encourages unity, and tells believers to follow the Christian path.

THE FIRST CHRISTIANS
For some time, Paul taught in the city of Antioch in Syria, where this church was built many years later. Paul sometimes referred to Jesus as Christ, meaning "the Anointed One," so from this time on believers became known as Christians.

EASTERN EMPEROR
Justinian I, a Christian emperor, ruled the Eastern, or Byzantine, empire from 527 to 565. He encouraged religious tolerance, tried to make peace between the rival Christian sects that existed at the time, and built churches in his capital city of Constantinople (now Istanbul, Turkey).

Coin depicting Justinian I

CONSTANTINE THE CONVERT
In 312, Constantine I became emperor of Rome. The following year, he became a Christian and passed the *Edict of Milan*, which proclaimed that Christians should be tolerated, not persecuted. The faith could now spread with ease across the vast Roman empire.

Coin depicting Constantine I

SAINT PAUL'S LEGACY
Ever since Saint Paul went on his journeys, Christians have traveled around the world preaching the faith. Much of this missionary activity took place in the 19th century, with Europeans like Charles Creed preaching in countries such as New Zealand, as pictured here.

The Bible was actually written by many different people. The books of the Old Testament were written by unknown scribes over hundreds of years. The authors of the New Testament were early Christians. Scribes later made copies of these original texts by hand using quill pens.

Quill pens and ink horns

God's book

THE CHRISTIAN BIBLE consists of more than 60 separate books written over many centuries. These books are divided into two main groups. The Old Testament contains the history and sacred writings of the Jewish people before the time of Jesus, which are sacred to Jews as well as to Christians. The New Testament deals mainly with Jesus and his early followers. The original texts (the Old Testament written in Hebrew and Aramaic, and the New in Greek) were translated into modern languages by biblical scholars in the 20th century (pp. 34–35).

Mosaic of the creation of the birds, Monreale Cathedral, Sicily

THE FIRST FIVE
The first five books of the Bible describe the creation of the universe and tell stories of the earliest Jewish ancestors. One of the most important stories relates how Moses received the Tablets of Law, or Ten Commandments, from God. It is sometimes claimed that Moses was the author of these books.

GETTING HISTORICAL
Many of the Old Testament books are historical, following the fate of the Jewish people over hundreds of years. These historical writings describe events in the lives of notable kings, such as Solomon, who was famously visited from afar by the Queen of Sheba and her entourage.

HOLY PLACE
Built by King Solomon, the Temple in Jerusalem was the holiest of all places to the Jews. It was destroyed by the Babylonians, but the Jews eventually restored it. In the Roman period, the Temple was rebuilt again by Herod the Great. Luke's Gospel describes Jesus visiting this temple as a boy.

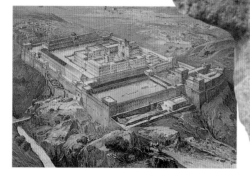

Artist's impression of Solomon's Temple in the time of Christ

2,500-year-old carved head of a woman from Sheba

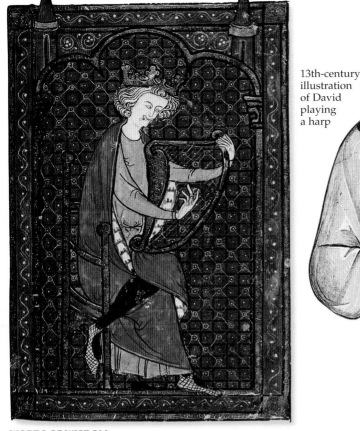

13th-century illustration of David playing a harp

THE WORDS OF THE PROPHETS

A large number of Old Testament books contain the sayings of prophets, such as Jeremiah, Isaiah, and Ezekiel. These men brought messages from God, telling people about God's will in relation to everything from everyday life to the future of the Jewish people. To early Christians, many of the prophets' words seemed to predict the coming of Jesus.

Depiction of Jeremiah from a 12th-century wall painting from Cyprus

Illustration of Paul's death from a 12th-century manuscript

WORDS OF WISDOM

The wisdom books are a group of Old Testament books written in various styles and on a range of subjects. The Psalms (originally said to have been written by King David) contain poetry praising God; the Proverbs consist of pithy, instructive sayings; and other books, such as Job, discuss human suffering.

13th-century illustration of Jonah and the fish

STORY WITH A MORAL

God told the prophet Jonah to visit the city of Nineveh to persuade the people to repent their sins. When Jonah refused, God sent a storm. Jonah was thrown overboard from his ship, and was swallowed by a great fish. When the fish finally spewed Jonah onto dry land, the prophet went straight to Nineveh.

WORK OF GOD

The later books of the New Testament are concerned mostly with the work of Jesus' followers, who carried on his mission after the Resurrection. This work is described both in the book of Acts and in the various epistles (letters) written by early church leaders such as Saint Paul.

SEEING TOGETHER

The first four books of the New Testament—the Gospels—tell the story of Jesus' life, crucifixion, and resurrection. The Gospels of Matthew, Mark, and Luke are very similar and are known as the "synoptic" (seeing together) Gospels. These were probably written soon after A.D. 65. John's Gospel is thought to have been written at the end of the first century.

Luke, the winged ox

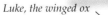

John, the eagle

The symbols of the evangelists, or writers of the Gospels, by modern artist Laura James

Matthew, the angel

Mark, the lion

Continued on next page

Early Bible texts

The books of the Bible were first written down by hand in the local languages of the eastern Mediterranean—Hebrew, Aramaic, and Greek. When different scribes copied out the texts, small variations occurred. The books were then translated into other ancient languages, such as Syriac. As a result, scholars translating the Bible into modern languages have a range of different sources to refer to, which helps them to make their version as close as possible to the original.

GUIDANCE FROM GOD
The Hebrew Bible—the Torah plus other books of narrative, prophecy, and wisdom—also makes up the Old Testament of the Christian Bible. Jesus often referred to these ancient Jewish scriptures, calling them the Law or the Writings. The five books that make up the Torah are Genesis, Exodus, Leviticus, Numbers, and Deuteronomy. They are central to the Jewish faith, and Deuteronomy includes 613 commandments that Jews try to follow in their everyday lives.

Crownlike finials, or tips, indicate the importance of the Torah

Tik, or Torah case, used by Spanish, Middle Eastern, and North African Jews

COVER UP
In the west, the Torah is usually kept in a cloth covering called a mantle. This is often embroidered with religious symbols. On this mantle, the crown is the symbol of the Torah, the Hebrew writing reads "Crown of the Torah," and the lions represent Judah, one of the tribes of Israel.

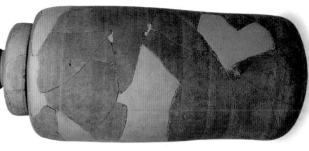

Pottery scroll jars

EARLIEST EXAMPLES
The Dead Sea Scrolls were found at Qumran in Jordan, on the edge of the Dead Sea, in 1947. They contain the earliest surviving manuscripts of most of the books of the Old Testament and also other texts in Hebrew, Greek, and Aramaic written down as early as the second century B.C.

HIDDEN TREASURE
The original owners of the Dead Sea Scrolls were members of a Jewish group called the Essenes. They kept the texts in large pottery jars. When their area was overrun by the Romans, the Essenes hid the Scrolls, which lay undiscovered for almost 2,000 years. Most of the Scrolls were damaged, but they have helped modern Bible translators, and taught scholars much about life in the first century A.D.

> *"The Spirit gives life; the flesh counts for nothing. The words I have spoken to you are Spirit and they are life."*
>
> JOHN 6:63
> Jesus to his followers

SIMPLY SYRIAC

Translations of the Bible into Syriac appeared very early—probably in the first or second century A.D. Called the *Peshitta* (meaning "simple"), the Syriac Bible has been used ever since in churches in Syria and neighboring areas, and was the basis for translations into Persian and Arabic.

ALL GREEK

The Gospels were written in the first century B.C. in Greek, a language shared by many early Christians. By this time, the Old Testament had been translated into Greek as well. The Greek Old Testament, called the *Septuagint*, was the version used by the earliest Christian communities and referred to in the Gospels.

Continued on next page

The text of the Torah is written in Hebrew on a continuous scroll

Fourth-century Greek text of Saint John's Gospel

BOOK BINDER

Underneath the mantle, the Torah is bound with a cloth called a *mappah*. Beneath this band is the scroll containing the text of the Torah. This Hebrew text is read in all synagogues (Jewish places of worship) and Jews believe that, if they follow the Torah, they are following the guidance of God.

Later Bible texts

From the fourth to the 15th centuries, monks translated the Bible into Latin, the language of the Western church. But the Reformation (pp. 34–35) brought a new demand for vernacular (local or current language) Bibles. People have been translating the Bible ever since, and today's translators try to be as accurate as possible while using words and phrases that are familiar to ordinary people.

Illuminated Bible with Latin text

THE ONE AND ONLY
Several Latin translations of the Bible were made, but the most famous was the one called the Vulgate, made by Saint Jerome in the late fourth century at the request of the pope. In 1546, the Council of Trent, a meeting of church leaders, declared the Vulgate to be the only authentic Latin text of the Bible.

The text of the Gutenberg Bible is the Latin Vulgate translation

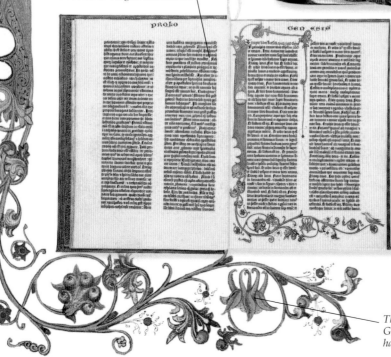

HANDY WORK
In the days before printing, monks wrote out the Latin texts of the books of the Bible by hand, often decorating the pages with beautiful illustrations. Psalters, which contain the words of the Psalms, were in great demand for use in services. This one includes an Old English translation between the lines of Latin text.

IN PRINT
Johannes Gutenberg (p. 34) produced the first printed edition of the entire Bible in Germany in 1455. Suddenly, it became possible to produce large numbers of Bibles quickly, bringing knowledge of the actual words of the Bible to more people than ever before.

The colored decorations in the Gutenberg Bible were added by hand after the text was printed

WILLIAM TINDALL

Illustrations help bring the text to life

GOOD NEWS

By the 20th century, most translations of the Bible seemed old-fashioned, and demand for Bibles written in modern languages grew. The *Good News Bible* and the *New International Version*, translated into modern English from the best Hebrew and Greek sources, met this need and have sold millions of copies.

Modern German Bible

AHEAD OF THEIR TIME

German theologians translated parts of the Bible into their native language throughout the Middle Ages. The whole Bible was translated by about 1400, but the church frowned on vernacular Bibles, and these were not widely available until after the Reformation (pp. 34–35).

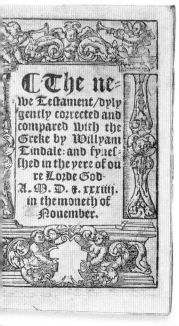

The different languages are divided into columns and blocks

A GOOD INFLUENCE

In the early 16th century, reformer William Tyndale wanted to translate the Bible into English. The English church would not allow this, so Tyndale moved to Germany, where he published his New Testament in English in 1525. This copy is a revised version, printed in 1534. It greatly influenced later Bible translators.

LOTS OF LANGUAGES

The interest in Bible translation, and the need to compare different texts, led to the production of polyglot Bibles, in which the text is printed side-by-side in several different languages. These pages come from an early polyglot Bible of 1516, with the text in Hebrew, Greek, Latin, and Arabic.

31

XXVI · PSALM · DAVID · PRIUSQUAM LINI

DNS ILLVMINATIO

DETSALVS MEA QUEMTIMEBO · DABO
DNS DEFENSOR UITAE MEAE AQUO TREPI
DUM ADPROPI ANT SUPER ME NOCENTES UT EDANT
CARNES MEAS QUI TRIBULANT ME INIMICI MEI
IPSI INFIRMATI SUNT ET CECIDERUNT ·
CONSISTANT ADUERSUM ME CASTRA NON TIME
BIT COR MEUM · SIINSURGAT IN ME PROELIUM
IN HOC EGO SPERABO ·
NAM PETII A DNO HANC REQUIRAM UT INHABITEM
IN DOMO DNI OMNIBUS DIEBUS UITAE MEAE · Teius
UT UIDEAM UOLUNTATEM DNI ET PROTEGAR A TEMPLO SCO
UM ABSCONDIT ME IN TABERNACULO SUO IN DIE MALO
RUM PROTEXIT ME IN ABSCONDITO TABERNACULI SUI
IN PETRA EXALTAUIT ME ·
UNC AUTEM EXALTAUIT CAPUT MEUM SUPER INIMI
COS MEOS CIRCUIBO ET IMMOLABO IN TABERNACULO
EIUS HOSTIAM IUBILATIONIS CANTABO ET PSAL. DICAM
XAUDI DNE UOCEM MEAM QUA CLAMAUI AD TE ·
MISERERE MEI ET EXAUDI ME ·

Heaven and Hell

12th-century icon from Saint Catherine's Monastery in Sinai, Egypt, depicting the Last Judgment

ALL CHRISTIANS believe in one eternal and almighty God, who exists as three beings—the Father, the Son, and the Holy Spirit. They believe that Jesus is the Son of God, that he lived on Earth as the son of the Virgin Mary, and that he was crucified and rose from the dead. Christians have faith that if they follow the teachings of Jesus and repent their sins they will be rewarded after death with everlasting life in Heaven— the traditional name for God's eternal kingdom. Its opposite, the place or state without God, is known as Hell.

14th-century painting of the Holy Trinity by Andrei Roublev

THREE IN ONE
The idea of the Holy Trinity, the one God who exists as three beings, is one of the deepest mysteries of Christian faith. God the Father is the almighty creator of the universe. God the Son is Jesus, God made human. God the Holy Spirit is God's power on Earth. The Bible describes Jesus as sitting at God's right hand in Heaven.

This medieval illustration shows angels blowing their trumpets as the dead rise from their graves

LAST JUDGMENT
Christians look forward to a time when Jesus will return to Earth. They believe that he will come again in glory to judge the living and the dead. Jesus will reward the righteous with eternal life, and the kingdom of God will truly exist and have no end.

Angel carrying a golden censer

Ivory counter showing human figures fighting off the demons of Hell to ascend to Heaven, 1120

IN HEAVEN
For some, Heaven is a literal place, a paradise where God dwells. Others emphasize that Heaven is not a place, but a state of being with God forever. Catholics (pp. 28–31) believe that a person's soul goes first to a third place, called Purgatory, where it is purified before entering Heaven.

WINGED MESSENGERS
The Bible refers to angels as spiritual beings who live with God in Heaven. They act as messengers, bringing God's words and judgments to people on Earth and providing spiritual guidance. The Bible gives few clues about what angels look like, but they are traditionally portrayed as winged beings with human bodies.

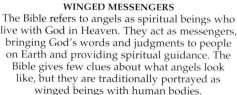

JACOB'S LADDER

The life of Jacob, one of the ancestors of the people of Israel, is described in the Book of Genesis. Jacob had a dream in which he saw a ladder connecting Heaven and Earth. As Jacob watched angels passing up and down the ladder, God spoke and promised that the land where he slept would one day belong to him and his descendants.

Relief of Jacob's ladder, west front of Bath Abbey, England

Angel carrying a casket that may contain saintly relics (pp. 42–43)

Angel carrying a model church

Angels are often portrayed with shining, golden wings

THE FALL OF SATAN

According to the Book of Revelation, Satan— a member of the highest rank of angels, the archangels—started a war with God. As a result he was thrown out of Heaven and started his own evil kingdom in Hell. Some Christians believe Hell to be a place of pain, where Satan and his demons torture the souls of the damned, forcing them to endure everlasting fire.

DEVILISH DEPICTIONS

Since medieval times, artists have portrayed Satan and his demons as grotesque creatures, human in form but with horns, tails, and cloven hoofs. Most Christians today are less concerned with the appearance of Satan and Hell, and are more likely to think of the torture of Hell as the agony of an existence without the love of God.

Modern Mexican stamp depicting a devil

LOTERIA DE
MEXICO 1998 99
20¢

EL DIABLITO
G. NORMA / C. VERGARA   TIEV

Catholicism

PAPAL SYMBOL
The papal symbol of the keys can be seen on Catholic buildings in many places around the world. This example is on the Hospital de los Venerables in Seville, Spain.

THE ROMAN CATHOLIC CHURCH is the largest of the Christian churches. Catholics place special stress on the Eucharist, or Mass (pp. 52–53), and are expected to go to Mass every Sunday. One distinctive feature of Catholic worship is commemoration of the saints. There is also a stress on devotional practices such as praying the rosary (p. 30) and making pilgrimages to shrines (pp. 42–43). In addition to the New Testament, Catholics are guided in their lives by the teachings of the church, which produces instruction on a range of topics from social justice to the church's contact with other faiths.

Censer stand is shaped like a crozier (p. 31)

Golden angels face into the center of the monstrance

DISPLAY CASE
This vessel, known as a monstrance, is used to display the host (the consecrated bread used during Mass). It consists of a glass-covered compartment surrounded by a metal frame with outward-spreading rays. It is used when the host is carried in processions, during a service called Benediction, and when the host is displayed for the purposes of devotion.

CHARTRES CATHEDRAL
Combining magnificent Gothic and Romanesque features along with over 200 stained glass windows, Chartres cathedral is often called the greatest in Europe. The cathedral was begun in 1020, destroyed by fire in 1194, and rebuilt in the mid-13th century.

CREATING AN ATMOSPHERE
Incense is used widely in the Catholic church. It is burned in a vessel called a censer—a pierced metal container hung on chains. When the censer is swung gently from side to side, sweet-smelling smoke comes out of the holes in the top of the vessel.

Baroque confessional box from Vienna in Austria

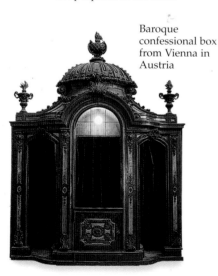

CONFESSIONS
Catholics are expected to confess their sins regularly to a priest, who sits in a boxlike structure called a confessional. The priest acts as an intermediary between God and the sinner, and pronounces God's willingness to forgive. The sinner may be asked to perform a penance—an action to show that they are truly sorry for their sin.

The lid lifts up so that the censer can be filled

Bird's-eye view of an incense boat

Benedictine monk sprinkling holy water

Aspergillum

Incense boat

Charcoal

Incense

The pope

The Catholic church is led by the pope, whom Catholics believe to be the direct successor of the disciple Peter— the first pope. Because Peter's authority came directly from Jesus, Catholics believe the pope's decisions on faith and morality to be infallible. The pope's teachings, explained in his letters and other documents, therefore have a huge influence on Catholics all over the world.

TIME TO BURN
Incense, which may be kept in an incense boat, is burned by being put into a censer along with hot charcoal. Incense is often used in the procession during which the priest enters the church. It may also be used at other times, such as the elevation of the host during Mass.

BADGE OF OFFICE
The ring is one of the pope's badges of office. This one belonged to Eugenius IV (pope from 1431 to 1437). In those days, popes were famed for their fine robes and jewelry. Modern popes are more often known for their moral guidance and wide contacts with the world's churches.

SOLEMN RITES
Water that has been blessed may be sprinkled during solemn rites such as blessings, exorcisms (the banishing of evil spirits), and burials. People may also be sprinkled with holy water during Mass. The sprinkling device, called an aspergillum, is a rod tipped with a bulb or brush.

CATHOLIC HEADQUARTERS
As well as being leader of the church, the pope is the Bishop of Rome, and lives in the Vatican City— a tiny independent state within Rome itself. The Vatican City is the headquarters of the Catholic church and contains Saint Peter's Basilica, the main church in the Catholic world.

Continued on next page

Leadership and spirituality

The leadership of the Catholic church is provided by both the pope and a hierarchy of clergy—archbishops, bishops, and priests. Bishops and priests lead by spiritual example, and also by teaching their flock about all areas of the Catholic faith. It is their job to educate members of the Catholic church on everything from the meaning of Mass (pp. 52–53) to the importance of prayer and reverence for the Virgin Mary.

14th-century bishops wearing full vestments

STATUS SYMBOLS
Miters, pointed headdresses with two ribbons hanging at the back, are worn by bishops, archbishops, and abbots (p. 48). They are usually decorated with religious symbols or scenes. The miter's tall shape is a sign of its wearer's status, the highest form of sacred ministry below that of the pope.

Depiction of the Annunciation

14th-century designs for miters

Mary being crowned

A BISHOP'S WORK
A bishop oversees the churches and priests in his diocese. He preaches, writes advisory letters to the local clergy, and directs the training of priests and the religious instruction given in Catholic schools. Bishops also belong to local or national groups called Bishops' Conferences, which meet to discuss collective policies.

PRAYING THE ROSARY
Catholics use rosaries as an aid to prayer. Three different prayers—the *Hail Mary*, the *Our Father* or *Lord's Prayer*, and the *Glory to the Father*—are repeated as the person meditates on the key stages of the Christian story. The rosary beads are used to count the prayers.

Rosary with medals showing saints for contemplation

Jesus raising his hand in blessing

14th-century French miter showing the coronation of the Virgin

PRIESTLY JEWELS
This chain was worn by a priest in 15th-century Italy. Modern priests rarely wear elaborate regalia like this, but they share the roles and values of their predecessors. Catholic priests must be male and are usually unmarried. They celebrate the sacraments, preach, provide instruction in the faith, and care spiritually for the people in their parish, or district.

Link made of gilded bronze

Sapphire mounted in chain

Pendant with nativity scene

Medieval crozier used by a bishop

Virgin Mary

Angel Gabriel

Enameled and gilded decoration

THE BLESSED VIRGIN MARY
Catholics regard the Virgin Mary with special devotion, and scenes from her life appear on many works of religious art, as well as on vestments and everyday objects. The Catholic church teaches that Mary was free from original sin and that at the end of her life on Earth she was taken up, body and soul, into Heaven—an event referred to as the Assumption. Because Mary is so revered, several festivals associated with her are held throughout the church year.

White roses of the Virgin Mary

"Hail Mary, full of grace, the Lord is with you; blessed are you among women, and blessed is the fruit of your womb, Jesus."

THE HAIL MARY

Madonna and Child, painted wood, c. 1320 Gothic

31

The Orthodox church

THE FORM OF CHRISTIANITY that is strongest in Eastern Europe and western Asia is known as the Orthodox church. It developed between the 9th and 11th centuries as a result of a split between Eastern and Western Christians, and claims to be closest to the faith as originally practised by Jesus' disciples. Like the Catholics, Orthodox Christians recognize several sacraments and venerate the Virgin Mary, but they do not recognize the authority of the pope. They place a heavy stress on holy tradition as revealed through the Bible and the collective decisions and teachings of the early church leaders.

ORTHODOX CHURCHES
The Orthodox church is a group of individual churches, each led by a patriarch, or senior bishop. Saint Basil's Cathedral in Moscow, Russia, with its striking onion domes, is under the leadership of the Patriarch of Moscow and all Russia.

Orthodox priests often have long beards and long hair

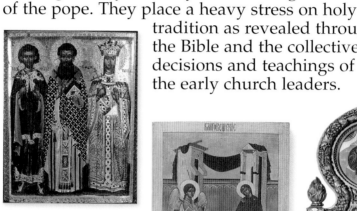

Greek icon showing three saints

HOLY FOCUS
Icons—usually small paintings of Jesus, Mary, or the saints—play a key part in Orthodox worship. Orthodox Christians see icons as reminders that God became human in the form of Jesus. They use them to help focus their prayers and devotions.

Russian annunciation icon

Portable icon designed to be worn as a pendant

The nails in Christ's hands are clearly visible

Crucifix icon from the Crimean War

ROYAL DOORS
In Orthodox churches, the sanctuary (the area containing the altar) is hidden by a screen called the iconostasis. The screen has a pair of doors called the royal doors, which are frequently beautifully decorated. These royal doors from the Russian Orthodox church in London, England, are decorated with images of the annunciation and the evangelists.

THE HEART OF THE MATTER
Orthodox priests must be more than 30 years old, and they are allowed to be married. The celebration of Holy Communion (pp. 52–53), usually referred to as the Liturgy, is at the heart of their work. Orthodox Christians believe that, during the Liturgy, God is especially present in the wine.

PORTABLE ICONS
Although the main place to display icons is in church, Orthodox Christians also use portable icons. These can be carried in processions, hung at shrines by the roadside, or used at home to help concentrate the mind during private prayer. Portable icons and similar items like this crucifix are especially popular in Russia.

OIL OF GLADNESS
When infants are baptized in the Orthodox church the priest immerses them three times in the font before anointing them with the "oil of gladness." The priest then performs the ceremony of chrismation, anointing the child on the head, eyes, nose, ears, and mouth. Chrismation in the Orthodox church is the equivalent to the Western ceremony of confirmation (p. 58).

ORTHODOX MONASTICISM
Monasticism (pp. 44–47) began in the East, in areas such as Egypt and Syria, and is still an important part of Orthodox religious life. Orthodox Christians believe that the presence of the Holy Spirit is revealed in the lives of monks and nuns. The most famous Orthodox monasteries are on Mount Athos in Greece, a monastic republic where monks have lived since the 10th century.

Stoles were originally made of wool to symbolize the flock for which priests are responsible

The crozier symbolizes the priest's power over his flock

Cuff symbolizes the power of God's right hand

BISHOP'S BUSINESS
All bishops are equal in the Orthodox church. They do have an overall leader— the Patriarch of Constantinople (Istanbul)—but he has no authority over the others. The main authority comes from synods, or meetings, of bishops held in each of the Orthodox churches to make decisions on matters affecting the church as a whole. Orthodox bishops are not permitted to marry, so bishops begin their calling as monks, not priests.

Orthodox bishop's vestments

The Reformation

During the 14th and 15th centuries, many people in Europe were worried that the Catholic church was becoming corrupt. In the early 16th century three men—Martin Luther from Germany, Ulrich Zwingli from Switzerland, and John Calvin from France—spearheaded the reform of the church across Europe. In the movement now known as the Reformation, they and their followers founded new, Protestant churches. These churches rejected the control of the pope and bishops and stressed the importance of the Bible and preaching God's word.

Medal from the 1500s depicting the pope as Satan

CHURCH ABUSES
Reformers objected to several practices in the Catholic church. One of the most widespread abuses of the church was the use of indulgences—the payment of money instead of doing penance for sins. Even some popes were corrupt, and objectors often portrayed them as devil-like figures.

Bar, to screw down the platen

Platen, used to press the ink onto the paper

The coffin is pushed beneath the platen

AGAINST CORRUPTION
This coin was made in honor of Jan Hus, a Czech priest who became a reformer in the early 1400s. He spoke out against the corruption of the church but, despite support from ordinary people, was prevented from preaching, excommunicated, forced to leave Prague, and eventually burned at the stake.

Ink ball, to spread the ink evenly

EARLY IDEAS
Englishman John Wyclif, a theologian and politician, began to demand church reform in the late 14th century. Many of his ideas—such as the denial of the pope's authority and the call for the Bible to be translated into modern European languages—were taken up by later reformers all over Europe. In this painting by Ford Madox Brown, Wyclif is reading from his translation of the Bible.

PRINTING PRESS
In the 1450s, craftsman Johannes Gutenberg of Mainz, Germany, invented a new method of printing. It enabled books to be printed quickly and cheaply. This major advance allowed the ideas of the Reformation to travel around Europe at great speed.

VOICE OF REASON
Education developed rapidly at the time of the Reformation through the work of teachers like Desiderius Erasmus, shown here in a painting by Hans Holbein. His methods were different from Luther's passionate, revolutionary approach—he hoped to reform the church through reason and scholarship. Erasmus edited the Greek New Testament, which was a great help to the scholars who would later translate the Bible into modern European languages.

FAMOUS THESES
In October 1517, Martin Luther posted 95 theses (arguments against indulgences) on a church door in Wittenberg, Germany. He followed this with several books about reform. He argued that salvation came from God's grace through the individual's faith in Christ, and could not be bought.

Tympan, where the paper is put

MOTHER TONGUE
In 1549, the Archbishop of Canterbury, Thomas Cranmer, published the *Book of Common Prayer*—a church service book in English. It enabled English people to hold services in their own language for the first time. When England briefly returned to Catholicism, under Queen Mary I in 1553, Cranmer was executed.

Full- and pocket-sized copies of the *Book of Common Prayer*

CHURCH LEADER
In 1534, King Henry VIII forced the English church to break from Rome because the pope would not allow him to divorce his wife, Catherine of Aragon. Henry himself became leader of the English church, although, apart from his rejection of the pope, he remained Catholic in his beliefs. Despite this, he began the process that brought Protestantism to England.

Gallows, to support the tympan

Bolton Abbey, England

16th-century portrait of Henry VIII by Hans Holbein the younger

DISSOLUTION OF THE MONASTERIES
Henry VIII ordered his chief minister, Thomas Cromwell, to compile a report on the monasteries in England. Cromwell concluded that many were rich and corrupt, so Henry ordered all the monasteries to be dissolved (closed). He seized the wealth of the monasteries and gave many of their lands to his lords. Most of the monastery buildings, like Bolton Abbey, were left to become ruins.

Protestantism

Since the Reformation, many different Protestant churches have been founded, all stressing the Bible as the source of their beliefs, and many advocating that salvation comes by God's grace, which is given to the believer through faith. Protestant churches range from huge international organizations, such as the Methodist, Anglican (p. 52), and Lutheran (pp. 34–35) churches to smaller groups like the Quakers, Shakers, and Seventh Day Adventists.

PURE AND SIMPLE
Protestant church buildings, like the one pictured above, tend to be plain with little of the decoration so common in Catholic and Orthodox interiors. The seats are arranged so that everyone can hear the sermons (p. 54) and readings.

Woman in 17th-century Puritan dress

PERSECUTED PURITANS
The Puritans were 17th-century English Protestants who wanted to cleanse the church of elements that they saw as Catholic, or "Popish"—such as vestments and bishops. Puritans, who stood out because of their plain clothes, were persecuted at home, so many moved abroad.

Model of the *Mayflower*

Quaker meeting house, Cornwall, England

17th-century Quaker

The ship was only 132 ft (40 m) long

MOVING MEETINGS
The Quakers worship in unadorned buildings called meeting houses. A typical Quaker meeting is simple and does not follow a set pattern. There are periods of meditation and silence until the Holy Spirit moves one or more of those present to speak or pray.

FRIENDS OF SOCIETY
The Quakers, also known as the Religious Society of Friends, were founded during the 17th century in England by George Fox. They have no Creed (p. 52), no sacraments, and their ministers are not ordained (pp. 48–49). Quakers are committed to peace, equality, and other social improvements, and played a major role in the abolition of slavery.

The cramped accommodation below deck was home to 102 pilgrims for 67 days

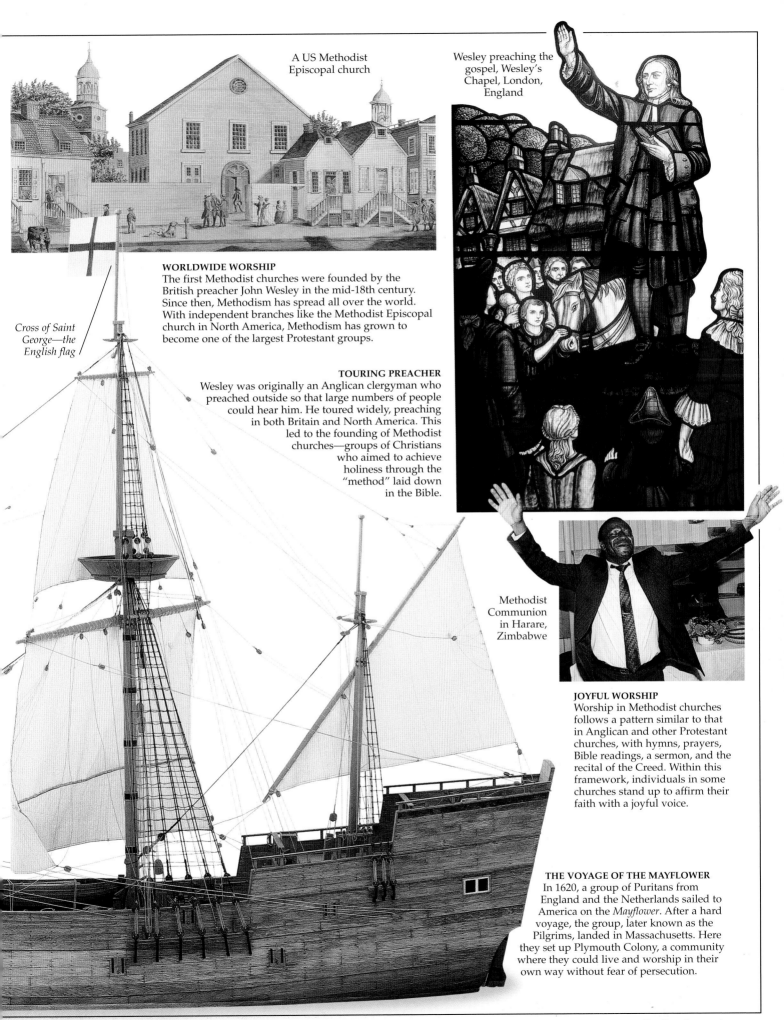

A US Methodist
Episcopal church

Wesley preaching the
gospel, Wesley's
Chapel, London,
England

*Cross of Saint
George—the
English flag*

WORLDWIDE WORSHIP

The first Methodist churches were founded by the
British preacher John Wesley in the mid-18th century.
Since then, Methodism has spread all over the world.
With independent branches like the Methodist Episcopal
church in North America, Methodism has grown to
become one of the largest Protestant groups.

TOURING PREACHER

Wesley was originally an Anglican clergyman who
preached outside so that large numbers of people
could hear him. He toured widely, preaching
in both Britain and North America. This
led to the founding of Methodist
churches—groups of Christians
who aimed to achieve
holiness through the
"method" laid down
in the Bible.

Methodist
Communion
in Harare,
Zimbabwe

JOYFUL WORSHIP

Worship in Methodist churches
follows a pattern similar to that
in Anglican and other Protestant
churches, with hymns, prayers,
Bible readings, a sermon, and the
recital of the Creed. Within this
framework, individuals in some
churches stand up to affirm their
faith with a joyful voice.

THE VOYAGE OF THE MAYFLOWER

In 1620, a group of Puritans from
England and the Netherlands sailed to
America on the *Mayflower*. After a hard
voyage, the group, later known as the
Pilgrims, landed in Massachusetts. Here
they set up Plymouth Colony, a community
where they could live and worship in their
own way without fear of persecution.

37

Continued on next page

Continued from previous page

Shaker meeting with leader Mother Ann Lee, 1774

THE SIMPLE LIFE
The Shaker movement reached its peak in the 19th century, and now there are very few Shakers. Members follow a simple lifestyle; they dress plainly, avoid alcohol and tobacco, and live in communities set apart from the outside world. Shakers are famous for the simple, well-made furniture that seems to sum up their way of life.

Shaker table and sewing chair

Salvation Army pin

Member of the Salvation Army saluting God

SEEKING SALVATION
Methodist minister William Booth founded the Salvation Army in the late 19th century, and it has since become a worldwide organization. The Salvation Army is famous for its outdoor preaching, its tuneful music, and its work to help the poor and needy. It preaches a Bible-based Christianity centered on the immortality of the soul and salvation by faith through grace.

RESPECT YOUR ELDERS
There are a number of Presbyterian churches around the world, and they share one key feature—they are governed by presbyters, or elders, who may be either ministers or lay people. This kind of organization was based on the ideas of reformer John Calvin. Worship is simple and centers on preaching and—as shown in this 19th-century painting—study of the scriptures.

Salvation Army song leader playing the cornet

Salvation Army tie

Modern Salvation Army man's hat

SOLDIERS OF GOD
The Salvation Army is organized along military lines. It is led by a "general," other church leaders are known as "officers," and members, or "soldiers," wear a distinctive uniform. Those who enroll sign a declaration of faith known as the "Articles of War." All members are entitled to bear the organization's red shield.

Victorian Salvation Army woman's bonnet

THE HOLY LIFE
Founded by a follower of the reformer Zwingli, Mennonites aim to live a life of holiness, set apart from the world in self-contained communities. They are pacifists, and they carry out relief work in many parts of the world.

Red shield badge

Modern Salvation Army woman's hat

Mennonite children in Belize

SEVENTH HEAVEN
Seventh Day Adventists, like this couple in Mozambique, believe that the time will come when they will be taken to Heaven for 1,000 years while Satan rules on Earth. At the end of this time, Jesus will return, destroy Satan, and create a new Earth. Adventists operate schools and a network of hospitals and clinics.

LIMITLESS WORSHIP
All Christians consider the work of evangelism, or spreading the Gospel, to be part of their faith. Many Protestants, like these in Guatemala, are very active evangelists. They often worship and preach outdoors, so their congregations are not limited by the size of a church building, and everyone who passes by can hear their message.

The Christian life

CHRISTIANS TRY TO FOLLOW Jesus' teachings and apply them to their own lives. All such believers are said to be part of the "community of saints." But some go to exceptional lengths for their faith, enduring suffering or persecution, or even becoming martyrs. Some of these men and women who have lived lives of special holiness are declared saints by the church. Saints are especially revered in the Catholic and Orthodox churches, where it is believed they can act as intermediaries between individual Christians and God.

The cross of Saint Brigid

FEEDING THE HUNGRY
Born in Ireland in the sixth century, Brigid became a nun and helped to spread Christianity by founding a monastery in Kildare. Brigid was famous for helping the poor, and was said to be able to make food multiply miraculously.

CHEATING DEATH
One of the many Christians who were persecuted by the Romans, Lucy remained true to her faith and gave away her possessions to the poor. The Romans were said to have tried to kill her by burning and by putting out her eyes. Lucy miraculously survived, and her eyes were restored. She was finally put to death by the sword.

Ivory relief of George and the dragon

Medieval gilded plaque of Saint Lucy

DRAGON SLAYER
George is thought to have been a third-century soldier from the eastern Mediterranean. The best-known story about him tells how a dragon was terrorizing the neighborhood and was about to devour the king's daughter. George said he would kill the monster if the people would believe in Jesus and be baptized. After killing the beast he would take no reward, but simply asked the king to help the church.

The palm is a symbol of the victory of the faithful over the enemies of the soul, and is often associated with martyrs

Eyes on a platter

SEEING THINGS
Hubert, the owner of this horn, lived in the eighth century and became a Christian after seeing a vision of the Crucifixion between the antlers of a stag while out hunting. From then on he devoted himself to converting others to Christianity in his native Belgium. He eventually became Bishop of Maastricht and Liège.

Plaster statue of Saint Joseph

A MAN OF INFLUENCE
Born in Algeria in 354, Augustine became one of the most influential theologians of all time. He was a lawyer and teacher before converting to Christianity in his thirties. His many books on subjects such as the Holy Trinity, charity, and the Psalms are still read today. He was also Bishop of Hippo in North Africa, as shown in this 15th-century painting.

16th-century painting of Saints Erasmus and Maurice

POPULAR SAINTS
Maurice, a soldier from Egypt, and Erasmus, a Syrian bishop, were martyred in the late third century. Although little is known of their lives, they were included in books of martyrs and became popular saints in the Middle Ages.

20TH-CENTURY SAINT
Italian Padre Pio was convinced of his "calling" as a child. When he became a Franciscan friar, he experienced visions of Jesus and received the stigmata—the miraculous appearance of wounds like those received by Jesus on the cross. Padre Pio endured his pain bravely, and devoted his life to prayer and serving God. He was declared a saint in 2002, 34 years after his death.

FAMILY LIFE
The family has a central role in Christian life. The Christian story begins with a family—Mary, Joseph, and Jesus—so it is seen by Christians as the ideal environment in which to raise children. This illustration shows a family walking to church on Christmas Eve.

JOSEPH THE PROTECTOR
As protector of the holy family, Joseph plays a vital part in the Christian story, and is especially revered in the Catholic church. Joseph is celebrated as the patron saint of fathers, carpenters, the dying, social justice, and the universal church.

HELPING HAND
Jesus told his followers to love their neighbors and give their wealth to the poor. Christians may follow these instructions through individual acts of kindness or through organizations that work to relieve suffering throughout the world.

Orphaned children helped by the Christian charity Tearfund

41

Continued on next page

Continued from previous page

Santiago de Compostela

The Virgin Mary
at Lourdes

PILGRIMAGE PLACES
Compostela in Spain and Lourdes in southwestern
France are two of Europe's best-known pilgrimage sites.
Compostela is said to be the burial place of Saint James,
one of Jesus' disciples. Lourdes is a more recent shrine,
the place where Saint Bernadette had a series of visions
in the 19th century, and where many apparently
miraculous healings have taken place.

Pilgrimages and relics

A pilgrimage is a journey to a place of religious
significance. Many Christians, especially Roman
Catholics, go on pilgrimages. They do so for
various reasons—to visit places that are important
for their faith, as an act of penance for their sins,
to ask for help, or to give thanks to God. The
most popular pilgrimage destinations are shrines.
A shrine is a place linked to a particular saint,
often housing their relics, or remains. Many sick
people make pilgrimages to shrines such as
Lourdes in the hope of a miraculous cure, but
pilgrims are just as likely to travel in search
of spiritual growth as physical healing.

*Crown of semi-
precious stones*

*Head is made of
silver, but gilding
gives it a golden
color*

*Ornate outer
case for the relics
of Saint Eustace*

*The base of
the casket is
decorated with
holy figures*

*The top lifted
off to reveal
the remains
stored within*

*Wooden inner
case—the true
receptacle for the
relics of Saint Eustace*

INSIDE STORY
This elaborate
reliquary was
made in about
1240 to hold
remains, which
included some of
the bones of Saint Eustace, an early
Christian who converted to the faith after
seeing a vision of the Crucifixion. The shining
metal outer covering and wooden inner box
did not contain Saint Eustace's whole skull,
but held a number of bones, which were
said to belong to several different saints.

CHAUCER'S PILGRIMS

In medieval England the shrine of Saint Thomas Becket at Canterbury was the most popular place of pilgrimage. The poet Geoffrey Chaucer wrote a long poem called *The Canterbury Tales*, made up of a series of stories told by a group of pilgrims as they traveled on horseback from London to Canterbury.

The Prioress

The Knight

The Man at Law

The Wife of Bath

The Squire

BECKET'S BONES

Thomas Becket was Archbishop of Canterbury in England during the reign of Henry II in the 12th century. When Becket fell out with the king, four of Henry's knights murdered him in Canterbury Cathedral. A shrine was soon built in the cathedral, and Becket's remains were kept in this beautiful casket.

Pewter badge of Saint Thomas Becket

Scallop-shaped ampulla, or flask, for holy water

One of the king's knights slices off Becket's head

Fragments of bone, wood, and fabric are beautifully displayed

MARK OF THE PILGRIM

In the Middle Ages, people often wore badges to show that they had been on a pilgrimage. The scallop shell, originally the badge of Compostela but later worn by pilgrims to any shrine, was the most common, but many places had their own badges.

INTO BATTLE

This reliquary, said to contain saintly bones, was carried into battle by the Abbot of Arbroath Abbey in Scotland. The occasion was the Battle of Bannockburn in 1314, when the Scottish, under their leader Robert Bruce, defeated the English.

TREASURED REMAINS

Relics do not have to be actual human remains. Fragments of objects that played a part in the Christian story are also revered. This collection of tiny relics, kept at a British Benedictine abbey, is said to include fragments of the cross, Jesus' crib, and the veil of the Virgin Mary, as well as relics of several saints.

Cross surrounded by pearls

Pieces of bone set in gold

PORTABLE RELICS

In the Middle Ages, some people carried holy relics around with them, in the hope that the remains would bring them closer to God. This small reliquary holds tiny pieces of the bones of saints, together with a small cross set among pearls. The use of gold and pearls in the reliquary reflects the high value of the items it contains.

Monks and nuns

FOR HUNDREDS OF YEARS, some Christians have felt the need to live separately from the rest of society, in special communities devoted to serving God. Such communities are called monasteries, and their inhabitants—monks or nuns—live a life that is harsher and stricter than normal. They make solemn vows to God of poverty, chastity, and obedience—promising to give up personal possessions and sexual relations and to obey both the head of the monastery (the abbot or abbess) and the set of rules by which they live. Monasticism plays an especially important part in the Catholic and Orthodox churches.

NUN AND MONK
In the Middle Ages, new orders of monks and nuns were often founded because people felt the need to live by stricter rules than those governing other monasteries. Members of different orders, like this Servite nun and Slavonic monk, can often be distinguished by the color of their clothes.

Modern-day Coptic monk

DESERT FATHERS
Monasticism began in Egypt in the third century, when men such as Saint Antony withdrew to the desert to live as hermits. These "desert fathers" eventually joined to form monasteries, and their traditions are carried on today by members of the Coptic church.

A SIMPLE LIFE
Saint Benedict wrote his rule at the monastery of Monte Cassino, Italy, in the 6th century. The rule imposes a simple life dominated by worship, prayer, reading, and work. It was adopted widely, and there are still a number of Benedictine monasteries today.

Church

Cloister gives access to main buildings and provides space for private study

Chapter house, where regular meetings are held

Refectory, where meals are taken

Herb and vegetable gardens

Gatehouse provides an entrance to the monastery

Dormitory, where the monks or nuns sleep

Outer wall cuts off building from the outside world

Infirmary, where the sick are treated

INSIDE A MONASTERY
A monastery has to provide somewhere for its monks or nuns to live, work, and worship. Traditionally, the main buildings are arranged around a courtyard called the cloister to one side of the church. These main buildings include a place to sleep, a place to eat, and a place in which to hold meetings. Fields and gardens for growing food are usually situated beyond the main complex.

THE WORK OF GOD

The most important activity for a monk or nun is regular religious observance at set hours of the day. Saint Benedict called this the "Work of God," but it is also known as the divine office. Everyone in the monastery meets eight times every day to pray, read lessons from the Bible, and sing hymns and Psalms.

FIGHTING MONKS

In the Middle Ages there were specialized orders of "fighting monks," who lived by monastic rules and gave armed protection to pilgrims in the Holy Land. This gunpowder flask bears the emblem of one such order, the Knights of Saint John.

15th-century monastic service book

Poor Clares—
Franciscan nuns

PRIVATE PRAYER

Individual worship plays a vital part in the daily life of all monks and nuns. These Franciscan nuns—known as Poor Clares after their founder, Saint Clare— are praying the rosary. Some orders count their prayers using knots on a piece of rope instead of rosary beads.

DIVINE LIGHT

Several of the "hours" of the divine office are celebrated when it is dark. Matins takes place at 2 AM, vespers during the evening, and compline before bedtime. Traditionally, worship at such times had to be celebrated by candlelight. The candles would also have reminded those taking part of the idea of Jesus as a divine light shining in the world.

Benedictine monk in quiet contemplation

HOLY READING

Benedictine monks are encouraged to read the Bible (and other religious writings) in a devotional, contemplative way to bring them into close communion with God. This activity, known as *Lectio Divina* (holy reading), does not involve analyzing the text, as some Bible-reading does. The reader should simply absorb the words and allow God's message to filter through.

Continued on next page

Continued from previous page

Lemon balm

Marjoram

Lungwort

Feverfew

HEALING HERBS
In the Middle Ages, monks grew plants like feverfew, lungwort, lemon balm, and marjoram to make medicines for ailments such as headaches and respiratory disorders. The monks wrote down their discoveries about the healing powers of plants in books called herbals. Herbs are still grown alongside other food plants in many monastery gardens today.

Everyday life and work
Although the divine office and prayer are at the heart of monastic life, monks and nuns are also expected to work hard to support themselves and their community. Monasteries often try to be as self-sufficient as possible, with many producing their own food, and some making items for sale. With their atmosphere of quiet contemplation, monasteries have always been centers of learning. In the Middle Ages, they provided Europe's only education and health services, and today many monks and nuns still teach in schools. They may also work in the wider community, giving aid to the sick, poor, and needy.

Benedictine monks in the refectory

FOOD FOR THOUGHT
In most monasteries, the monks or nuns eat together at long tables in a large communal refectory, or dining room. The food is simple but nourishing. Religious devotion even continues at meal times—everyone is expected to eat in silence while one of their number reads passages from the Bible.

SCENTED SERVICES
Incense—a substance that makes a sweet scent when it is burned— is used widely during services in both the Catholic and Orthodox churches. Some monasteries make incense, both for use in their own church and for sale to raise money.

Raw olibanum gum

Ground raw olibanum gum

Finished incense

Rubber gloves provide protection from the highly concentrated oil

1 NATURALLY SWEET
The naturally sweet-smelling raw olibanum gum is ground into smaller pieces. The monk then measures out a small amount of concentrated perfume oil and mixes this thoroughly with the ground gum.

2 DRYING OUT
The monk places shovels of the scented, ground gum into a large, wooden tray with a wire bottom and spreads it out evenly. He leaves the incense mixture until it is dry and then packs it up ready for sale.

Wafer press and wafers decorated with Christian symbols

FLAT BREAD
In many churches, specially made wafers—traditionally manufactured in monasteries—are used instead of ordinary bread during Communion (pp. 52–53). The process starts with a bread dough mix. This is pressed into thin sheets, often marked with a Christian symbol, and cut into small disks. The finished wafers are then packaged and supplied to churches all over the world.

FAR FROM HOME
Many monks and nuns travel long distances to take part in aid programs in areas that are affected by drought, war, famine, or other disasters. Members of monastic orders help to save lives and bring education to areas where there are no public schools.

Nun distributing cooking oil in Rwanda

The text is in Latin and is beautifully decorated

The desk slopes to make writing for long periods more comfortable

The nun studies the honeycomb to see if it is ready for harvesting

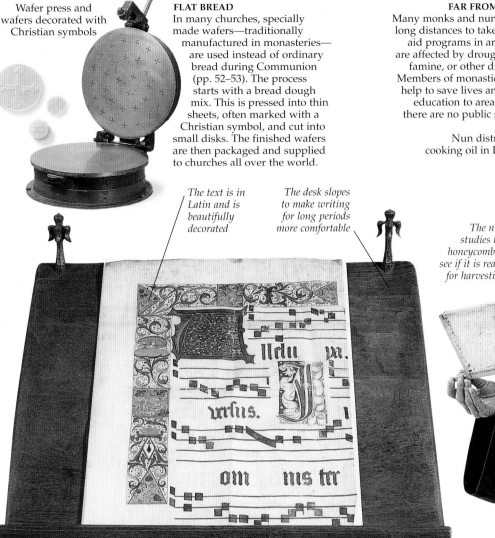

Monastic scribe's desk

WRITING FOR GOD
In the Middle Ages, monks and nuns were among the few people who produced books. They wrote out each page by hand and decorated them to produce results like this beautiful music manuscript. Today, some monks preserve these ancient skills, while others are notable scholars. They write books on subjects such as the Bible, theology, and the history of the church.

Wax tablet for writing holy passages on

SWEET AND SYMBOLIC
Honey is an ancient Christian symbol that reminds the faithful of the sweetness of Jesus' words. This Franciscan nun has learned the valuable skill of beekeeping, providing a nutritious food source for her sisters and beeswax for making candles. Many monks and nuns sell any honey and wax they do not use themselves to members of the public.

The angel's banner says "With the Lord a thousand years is a single day"

Plate made to commemorate the year 2000

CHRISTIAN EARTHENWARE
The pottery founded by the Benedictine monks of Prinknash Abbey in England produces simple wares for everyday use, and more decorative ceramics that are especially attractive to visitors. Their millennium plate bears a picture of an angel, a reminder that the year 2000 was, above all, a Christian event—the 2,000th anniversary of Jesus' birth.

The priesthood

HOLY LEADERS
This ancient ivory chesspiece shows a bishop—a senior Catholic, Orthodox, or Anglican clergyman who oversees the work of other priests.

Priests and ministers—their equal in many Protestant churches—provide spiritual teaching, celebrate the sacraments, and play the leading role in rituals and worship. They also care for people in their parish, or area—for example, by visiting the sick and caring for those with special needs. Being a priest is demanding, and most people who take on the role do so because they feel a spiritual "calling." In the Catholic and Orthodox churches, ordination, or admission, is a sacrament and is permanently binding, whereas in the Protestant churches it is not.

RELIGIOUS PRIESTS
An abbot is a priest who is the leader of a monastery. He and the monks in his charge are known in the Catholic church as "religious priests." The other members of the Catholic clergy—such as bishops and parish priests—are referred to as "secular priests."

Rear view of abbot's vestments

Miter shows that the wearer is an abbot

Early-20th-century silver crozier, carried only by higher members of the clergy

Cowl, or hood

Red cope worn on major feast days, such as Pentecost, Easter, and Christmas

Ornamental cross

Surplice, or alb, worn beneath cope

Habit, or tunic, worn beneath vestments

Benedictine abbot in ceremonial vestments

SIMPLE STYLE

The Anglican church allows both men and women to become priests, or vicars, as they are often called. Much of the time vicars wear simple clothes, such as a round clerical collar and plain shirt. For services they may wear vestments, the style of which can vary according to the occasion and their own views.

Clerical collars are sometimes referred to as "dog collars"

Confirmation

Eucharist

Anointing the sick

Baptism

SEVEN SACRAMENTS

The Catholic and Orthodox churches celebrate seven sacraments—rites that constitute a visible sign of the inward grace of God. The sacraments on this 15th-century altarpiece are ordination, confirmation, Eucharist, penance, anointing the sick, baptism, and marriage. Many Protestant churches recognize only two sacraments: baptism and Communion.

Gold trimmings add to the splendor of the outfit

Anglican vicar wearing everyday clothes

Anglican vicar dressed for Holy Communion

Saint Ignatius of Loyola

TEACHING PRIESTS

The Society of Jesus, or Jesuits, are an order of Catholic priests founded in the 16th century by former soldier Ignatius of Loyola. The Jesuits have always been committed to missionary work and education, and priests often teach in schools or universities. After his death in 1556, Ignatius of Loyola was made a saint.

IN UNIFORM

When celebrating the sacraments, priests wear special clothes called vestments. These garments are similar in design to those worn by early Christians in ancient Rome. They consist of several layers, which include a white tunic called an alb, a colored overgarment called a chasuble, and a long, scarflike stole.

The church

THE WORD CHURCH means a community of Christian believers, but it is also used to refer to a building in which Christians worship. Churches vary widely, but most have a large main space—often called the nave—for the congregation. Many churches also have a chancel or sanctuary, which houses the altar (p. 52); side chapels, used for private prayer; a vestry, where the priest prepares for services; and a space in which baptisms take place.

PRAYER IN PRIVATE
The earliest churches were often small and very simple in design. This sixth-century building in Ireland is an oratory, a place where someone can pray in private rather than a church for a large congregation. It has sloping stone walls, a single door, and no windows.

Ornate holy water stoup

HOLY WATER
In many churches there is a stoup, or basin, near the door. This contains holy water with which people can cross or sprinkle themselves as they enter the building, as a way of affirming their baptism (p. 58).

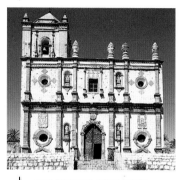

ALL SHAPES AND SIZES
There are many different church designs. The mission church at San Ignacio (above) and Saint George in the East (right) are in the baroque style, which uses decorative features adapted from buildings in ancient Rome. Both have a bell tower and a large door leading to the nave. Elaborate architecture like this is common in Catholic churches, but Protestant buildings tend to be plainer.

18th-century church, San Ignacio, Mexico

MAKING AN ENTRANCE
Church doorways are sometimes surrounded by statues of saints and biblical scenes, which remind people that they are entering a sacred building. This doorway is topped by a carving of the baby Jesus and the Magi.

Doorway to a 12th-century church in Loches, France

Carving of a bishop

Bell tower

Model of Saint George in the East church, London, England

Main entrance

Carving of Saint Peter

A WORLD OF HORROR
In the Middle Ages, builders often placed carvings of ugly faces, monsters, and other weird beasts on the outside walls of churches. People looking at these grotesque carvings knew that when they went inside the church they were leaving behind the world of horror and the evil that went with it.

GOSPELS IN GLASS
In ancient churches, stained glass was a way of teaching Bible stories to ordinary people, most of whom were not able to read or write. Christian symbols like this fish from Prinknash Abbey in Gloucestershire, England, are particularly popular in modern churches.

15th-century German altarpiece

FOCAL POINT
Behind the altar in many churches there may be an altarpiece. This is a screen, painting, or carved relief that focuses attention on the altar itself. An altarpiece may be decorated with scenes from the Bible, images of saints, or representations of everyday life, as in this example that shows a family caring for a newborn child.

Lectern Bible

CHURCH READINGS
The word of God is central to the Christian faith and Bible-readings are part of almost every service. Most churches keep a large Bible open on a stand called a lectern. Lecterns are often made in the shape of an eagle, the emblem of Saint John the Evangelist.

Medieval lectern

ELEVATED POSITION
The structure in which the priest or minister stands to preach the sermon (p. 54) is called the pulpit. It is generally raised so the preacher can be seen and heard by everyone in the congregation. In Catholic churches the pulpit is usually set to one side, but in Protestant churches it is often central—reinforcing the emphasis on the importance of God's word.

Portuguese pulpit with a spiral stairway

SITTING COMFORTABLY
In a Catholic church like this English monastic chapel, the congregation sits in pews in front of the altar, which is the main focus. In Orthodox churches the altar is hidden behind a screen and there are few seats, so most of the worshippers stand. Congregations in Protestant churches tend to sit facing the pulpit.

Holy Communion

The design on this kneeler combines the bread and wine with *chi* and *rho*, the first letters of the word Christ in Greek.

For most Christians, the church's supreme rite is the reenactment of the Last Supper, when participants receive the consecrated, or blessed, bread and wine. Catholics know this as the Mass or Eucharist, Orthodox Christians call it the Holy Liturgy, and Protestants may call it the Holy Communion or the Lord's Supper. In all churches, the bread and wine are identified with the body and blood of Jesus Christ. Protestants see the two elements as reminders of Jesus' sacrifice. Catholics believe that Christ's body and blood are actually present in the elements of the Mass.

THE ANGLICAN WAY
The various branches of the Christian church celebrate Holy Communion in different ways. These two pages show how Communion is celebrated in an Anglican church. The first part of the service focuses on the word (p. 54). It includes prayers, one or more Bible readings, a sermon, the Creed (the statement of belief in God), and the Peace ("The Peace of the Lord be always with you").

4 RECEIVE THE BREAD
The priest invites the congregation to take Communion, and prays that their bodies will be cleansed through Jesus' body. The priest then takes and eats part of the consecrated bread. (Some priests receive the bread after blessing the wine.)

1 TAKE THE BREAD
After the Peace, a hymn, and an offering, the priest's words recall the Last Supper. He takes the bread from the Communion table, which may also be referred to as the Lord's table or altar.

2 GIVE THANKS FOR THE BREAD
The priest gives thanks to God for the bread, echoing as he does so the description in the Gospels of how Jesus blessed the bread at the Last Supper.

3 BREAK THE BREAD
Again following the actions of Jesus at the Last Supper, the priest breaks the bread. This is so that those present may "share in the body of Christ."

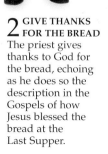

5 TAKE THE WINE
Next, the priest takes the wine from the Communion table. The wine is usually contained in a special goblet, or cup, called a chalice. The chalice represents the vessel that would have held the wine at the Last Supper.

The priest raises his right hand in a gesture of blessing

The priest offers the bread to the member of the congregation kneeling before him

9 GIVE THE WINE
Then members of the congregation take the wine from the chalice in turn. Afterward, they say a further prayer of thanksgiving before the final hymn, prayer, and blessing bring the service of Holy Communion to an end.

7 RECEIVE THE WINE
Raising the chalice to his lips, the priest receives the wine. He is now ready to offer Holy Communion to those members of the congregation who have come forward to take it.

8 GIVE THE BREAD
When enough bread for the congregation to share has been broken, it is distributed to those present. In some churches, the bread may take the form of small, unleavened wafers.

6 GIVE THANKS FOR THE WINE
The priest blesses the wine. By giving thanks in this way, he has prayed that the souls of both clergy and congregation may be washed with Jesus' "most precious blood."

HOLY CUP
This 16th-century chalice is made of silver, and is beautifully decorated with the heads of saints. Although similar chalices are still used today, in some churches, especially those with large congregations, tiny individual cups are handed around instead.

PRECIOUS PLATE
The consecrated bread at Holy Communion is placed on a plate, known as a paten, which usually matches the chalice. Because the bread and wine are so important, both the paten and the chalice are often made of precious metals, such as silver or gold.

Portable Communion set

Chalice

Bottle containing wine

Paten

Tin to hold Communion wafers

SMALL SCALE
Although the usual place to celebrate Holy Communion is in church, it may also take place elsewhere. If a priest or vicar is celebrating Holy Communion with a sick person, he or she will take a portable Communion set consisting of a box for consecrated bread or wafers, a bottle for wine, and a scaled-down paten and chalice.

THE WORD

Religious speeches known as sermons became popular in the Middle Ages, as shown by this 1491 woodcut, and are still a vital part of many church services. The preacher often takes a passage from the Bible as a starting point for the sermon, and uses it to explain a Christian message.

Ways to worship

COMMUNAL WORSHIP IS at the heart of the Christian faith, and many Christians come together regularly to praise God, confess their sins, and show that they are followers of Jesus Christ. Worship can involve all sorts of activities. Reading the Bible, singing hymns, songs and Psalms, praying, and listening to sermons are all aspects of Christian worship used in church services the world over. These services may vary widely in tone and mood, but most contain several of these key elements. For committed Christians, however, worship does not begin and end in church—they dedicate their whole life to God.

DAILY SERVICE

Medieval breviary

A breviary is a book used in the Catholic church that contains daily services for the canonical hours—services that are held at regular times each day. Each service consists of a short prayer, a hymn, three Psalms, a lesson, and final prayers. Modern breviaries contain services for morning, daytime, evening, and nighttime.

HOLDING CROSS

This simple cross is made of olive tree wood from the Holy Land, and is designed to be held in one hand during worship. Its rounded, smooth shape makes it comfortable and easy for a sick or elderly person to grip.

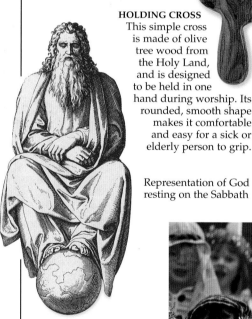

Representation of God resting on the Sabbath

THE SABBATH DAY

For thousands of years, the Jews have observed their Sabbath—a day set aside for rest and religious observance to mark God's day of rest after the creation—on a Saturday. The early Christians decided to make Sunday their Sabbath, and this day is still a day of rest in Christian countries.

POPULAR PSALMS

Books of Psalms called psalters, like this 700-year-old example, were some of the most beautiful volumes in the Middle Ages. Psalms are still sung, chanted, or spoken out loud today, and are widely used as the basis for popular hymns and prayers.

ANCIENT AND MODERN

Carols are songs that express religious joy, most widely sung at Christmas. Carols first became popular in the 15th century, but new ones are still being written, sung, and enjoyed alongside the old.

The words to the songs are in Latin

Antiphonal, or song book

Crossed keys are the symbol of Saint Peter

CHRISTIAN CUSHION

People usually kneel or bow their heads when they pray, and some churches provide cushions on which to kneel. These are often embroidered with Christian symbols or scenes. Adopting a special posture for prayer can help concentration, and shows reverence, or respect, when communicating with God.

BEAUTIFUL BOOKS

In medieval Europe many rich people owned a Book of Hours. These beautifully illustrated books contained the words of short religious services to be performed in church or recited at home as part of a person's private religious observance.

Carved angel from the altar at Saint Michael's Cathedral, Chicago

Selection of metal and wooden organ pipes

LET US PRAY

Christians pray for all kinds of reasons. They pray to give thanks to God for the creation and for the route to everlasting life given through Jesus Christ. They may also pray to ask for forgiveness for sins, and to ask for God's help in the lives of individuals, groups, or the world as a whole.

PERFECT HARMONY

This abbot from a Benedictine monastery is wearing a habit called a choir cowl. He is singing from an antiphonal, a book of songs designed to be sung by two groups during worship. The music of one group responds to that of the other in a kind of echo. The two groups, who may stand on either side of the church, combine in beautiful harmony.

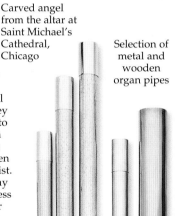

PIPED MUSIC

A vast instrument capable of a huge range of sounds, the organ has been used to accompany singing in churches for hundreds of years. A traditional organ works by blowing air into a series of pipes, which vary in size and so produce notes of different pitches. Each note is controlled by one of a series of keys and pedals, operated by the organist's hands and feet.

Modern organ

Christian calendar

THE CHRISTIAN YEAR is dominated by two major cycles, or groups of festivals. The first, at the beginning of the church year, starts with Advent and leads to Christmas. But, at the heart of the Christian calendar, is the observance of Jesus' crucifixion and resurrection. This begins with the period of Lent, followed by Holy Week, the mourning of Jesus' death on Good Friday, and the celebration of his resurrection on Easter Sunday. The other major Christian festival is Pentecost, which marks the gift of the Holy Spirit to Jesus' disciples.

Priest wearing colored stoles

CALENDAR COLORS
Many priests wear different colored vestments at different times in the church calendar. The colors vary, but red is often worn for Pentecost and green for the Sundays after Epiphany and Trinity, when the Holy Trinity is honored.

Tangerines and walnuts

GIFTS FOR THE GOOD
Epiphany, on January 6, marks the visit of the Magi to Bethlehem—the first time that Jesus was revealed to non-Jews. In Spain, children believe that the Magi come to give them presents. They put out fruit and nuts for "the Magi," who leave behind gifts for well-behaved children and candies that look like coal for those who have misbehaved.

Coal candies

Spanish girl with chocolate models of the Magi

German advent calendar

"Today in the town of David a Savior has been born to you; he is Christ the Lord."

LUKE 2:11
Angel of the Lord to the shepherds

American Christmas meal

COUNTDOWN TO CHRISTMAS
To most Christians, Advent is the period leading up to Christmas, including the four Sundays before December 25. During this season, Christians celebrate the arrival of John the Baptist, the coming of the Messiah, and Jesus' future second coming. Calendars offering a candy to eat on each day of Advent are traditional in many homes.

FESTIVE FUN
Jesus' birth is celebrated on December 25 in most branches of the Christian church. People attend joyful services, decorate their homes, exchange presents, and eat festive meals. In the West, a traditional Christmas dinner consists of roast turkey with a selection of vegetables and sauces.

VISUAL REMINDER
A crèche is a model of the stable where Jesus was born, featuring the holy family, shepherds, animals, and the magi. This example comes from El Salvador. Crèches are a good visual aid for teaching children about the Christmas story—and are a reminder to all of the Christmas message.

16th-century Italian Lent parade helmet

Palm leaf crown

A SOLEMN TIME

Mardi Gras is traditionally a time for people to confess their sins and use up rich foods before Lent—the 40-day period preceding Easter. Lent is a time of solemnity, penance, and devotion to God. It was originally a time of fasting, but today most Christians fast only on Ash Wednesday and Good Friday.

PALM SUNDAY

On the Sunday before Easter, Christians commemorate Jesus' entry into Jerusalem. People take part in processions carrying, wearing, and waving palm leaves and palm crosses. Palm Sunday marks the beginning of Holy Week, the time when people remember the events that led up to the Crucifixion.

Jesus reigning from the cross

Benedictine monk taking part in an Easter procession

A NEW LIFE

Easter is the feast of Jesus' resurrection. In church, priests read the Gospel story of the Resurrection and lead joyful prayers, hymns, and processions to celebrate the risen Christ. Eggs are seen as symbolic of Jesus' new life, and many people eat chocolate eggs or decorate real eggs at Easter time.

Pumpkin— a traditional harvest vegetable

GIVING THANKS

Harvest festival is not part of the official church calendar, but Christians in many places get together each year to give thanks for the produce of the land. People sing special hymns and bring produce to churches to be distributed to the poor and needy. Some seaside towns celebrate the "harvest of the sea" brought in by local fishermen.

Palm ring

LIFE AND DEATH

All Soul's Day, on November 2, is a popular Catholic festival. It is a day when people pray for the souls of the dead and put flowers on family graves. People in Mexico celebrate two Days of the Dead at this time of year. They exchange gifts like this sugar skull as reminders of death and the continuity of life.

Ethiopian boy in Palm Sunday dress

The cycle of life

As a Christian passes through the key stages of life, their relationship with the church develops. This development is marked with rites such as baptism (when a person enters into the church), confirmation (when they confirm their faith), marriage (when a couple are united in the eyes of the church), and funeral services (when a person dies). Baptism, together with confirmation and marriage in the Catholic church, is a sacrament, an outward sign of God's inward and spiritual grace.

Kneeling cushion with a design for a confirmation service

MAKING A COMMITMENT
When an infant is baptized, the parents and godparents make a commitment to Christianity on the baby's behalf. When old enough, the child confirms their faith. After a preparatory course, the candidate for confirmation vows to leave evil behind and to be a committed Christian. The bishop lays his hands on the candidate's head and blesses them.

The baby is dressed in white as a symbol of purity

Anglican priest baptizing a baby

Portable font filled with holy water

BORN AGAIN
In the Baptist church, and some other churches, people are baptized only when they are old enough to decide for themselves that they believe in God. In this "believer's baptism," the person confesses their faith and is completely immersed in water. The baptism symbolizes being washed clean and born again in Jesus.

THE BAPTISM OF JESUS
It is the baptism of Jesus by John the Baptist in the Jordan River that has led several Protestant churches to follow this practice. The total immersion is considered to be symbolic of Jesus' death, burial, and resurrection.

BABY BAPTISM
When an Anglican priest baptizes a baby, she brings the child to the font, reads from the Gospels, says a prayer, and addresses its carers about its Christian upbringing. She then baptizes the child, pouring holy water over its head and saying, "I baptize you in the name of the Father, and of the Son, and of the Holy Spirit." In the Catholic church, the baby is also anointed with consecrated oil, called chrism.

The bride traditionally wears a veil, a symbol of chastity

'TIL DEATH US DO PART

Christians see marriage as a lifelong partnership and some churches, such as the Catholic church, do not recognize divorce. A wedding is therefore both a happy event and a serious one. Weddings are full of symbolism. Orthodox couples, for example, are crowned with wreaths to show that they are rulers of their kingdom—the family.

Lilies are symbols of purity: they also represent the Virgin Mary

WEDDING CEREMONIES

Churches all over the world hold wedding ceremonies. These are joyful occasions often attended by many guests. The priest establishes that the couple are free to marry, vows and rings are exchanged, and the union is blessed.

The dove reminds couples of the presence of the Holy Spirit

Wedding kneeler

Ivory counter showing burial scene

Mourning brooches from the mid-1800s

CELEBRATING A LIFE

When someone dies, their body is placed in a coffin and taken to church, where mourners gather to celebrate the life of the deceased. Prayers, readings, and hymns remind mourners that the soul of the dead person will live on, and give thanks for this. Finally the body is either cremated or buried in a consecrated graveyard.

White wedding dresses have been popular since the 19th century

DEATH CEREMONIES

Funerals vary widely in style, from solemn and contemplative to noisy and expressive. Protestant funerals include prayers, Bible-readings, hymns, and a eulogy, or speech, commemorating the deceased before the burial or cremation. Catholics pray for the soul of the dead person and may hold a special Requiem Mass in their honor.

New Orleans jazz funeral

PUBLIC PRAYER
Many Christians pray at home, but people will also pray in public at times of trouble or prior to performing an important task. Before her race, this athlete asks God for help and dedicates her efforts to God.

Christian culture

ARTISTS, WRITERS, AND MUSICIANS have been responding to the Christian message for 2,000 years. Very early in the history of Christianity, people were decorating church walls and writing music for use during services. Soon, much of the art produced in the Western world was Christian, and as the faith spread around the world, its influence on art followed. There are fewer Christian artists today, but Christianity still influences both our art and lives.

"...in everything, by prayer and petition, with thanksgiving, present your requests to God."

PHILIPPIANS 4:6
Paul in his letter to the church at Philippi

We swear oaths in court, listen to gospel music, watch movies based on Bible stories, and see paintings, statues, and buildings that rework Christian subjects in exciting new ways.

SOLEMN PROMISES
In Christian cultures, the most solemn, binding promise is an oath sworn on the Bible, "by almighty God." A court official like this judge swears to do his job to the best of his ability. A witness in court swears to tell the entire truth.

The visual arts

From paintings and statues of Jesus to soaring cathedrals that seem to reach to the heavens, Christianity has had a huge impact on the visual arts. Most famous examples date from earlier times, but visual artists are still being inspired by the faith. Some make art to adorn churches, and others draw on Christian imagery to produce works for a wider public.

CHRIST OF RIO
Completed in 1931, *Christ the Redeemer* stands more than 100 ft (30 m) tall and overlooks Rio de Janeiro, Brazil. It was designed by artist Carlos Oswaldo and carved from soapstone, which, although quite soft, is resistant to weather damage. From the top of the rocky outcrop of Corcovado, the statue dominates the city and has become known the world over as a symbol of Rio.

The wings are tilted forward to give a sense of embrace

STEEL ANGEL
Antony Gormley's *Angel of the North*, which stands in Gateshead in England, has wings 175 ft (54 m) wide—similar in size to the wings of a jumbo jet. This modern angel, completed in 1998, is seen by thousands of travelers on the road and railroad line that pass the site. Made of a special steel that contains copper, the statue has a rich reddish-brown color that stands out against the sky.

GLASSY GLORY

Popular since the early Middle Ages, stained glass windows flood the interiors of many churches with beautiful colored light. This spectacular spiral window, leading the eye up toward the heavens, is a modern take on this old tradition. Installed in 1996 at Thanksgiving Chapel in Dallas, Texas, the *Glory Window* was designed by French artist Gabriel Loire.

UNDER CONSTRUCTION

Most of the world's cathedrals were finished long ago, but a few are still being built. Barcelona's vast cathedral of the Sagrada Familia (Holy Family) was designed by Catalan architect Antoni Gaudí. Construction began in the 1880s, but the huge building project continues to this day.

THE NINE SAINTS

Modern New York painter and illustrator Laura James is inspired by the art of Ethiopia, and in her painting of nine Ethiopian saints she hopes to introduce people to the history of this country. Christianity came to Ethiopia in the fourth century, so the artist has a long tradition from which to draw inspiration.

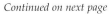

Continued on next page

ACTING WITH PASSION

In some parts of Europe, local people put on traditional plays enacting the story of the Passion—the events leading up to Jesus' crucifixion. In the village of Oberammergau in southern Germany, the Passion play has been staged regularly ever since the people escaped the plague in 1633. The play is now produced every ten years.

This scene is set in the disciple Simon's house

The performing arts

Music has been a part of Christian worship for centuries, and many composers in the Middle Ages were monks who spent their lives writing and singing church music. But from the beginning, religious music influenced other types of music, from extravagant choral pieces to dances and popular songs. Drama has also been influenced by Christianity for hundreds of years, and there are many famous movies and plays with religious themes.

The parting of the Red Sea

Moses

Rameses II

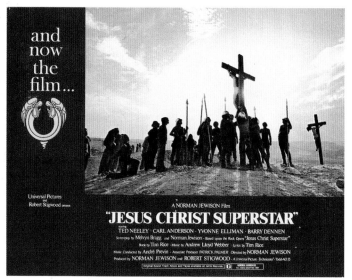

FROM STAGE TO SCREEN

The "rock opera" *Jesus Christ Superstar* was first staged in 1970, and made into a movie in 1973. With music by Andrew Lloyd Webber and words by Tim Rice, the production was one of the most popular 20th-century treatments of the Christian story.

"Shout for joy to the Lord, all the earth. Worship the Lord with gladness; come before him with joyful songs."

PSALM 100:1–2
A hymn of praise

EPIC MOVIE

The Ten Commandments—a movie created in 1956 by Hollywood director Cecil B. de Mille—tells how Moses led his people out of slavery in Egypt to their promised homeland. It features a huge cast, with Charlton Heston as Moses and Yul Brynner as Rameses II, and spectacular special effects, such as the parting of the Red Sea to let the Israelites pass.

SACRED SONGS

Sacred oratorios (a blend of solo and choral music) became popular in the 18th century. Among the most famous are J. S. Bach's two settings of the Passion story and G. F. Handel's *Messiah*. Handel wrote the piece in less than four weeks in 1741, and its portrayal of Jesus' life is still enjoyed by audiences today, especially around Christmas time.

Handel's original score of *Messiah*

Gospel choir performing in Washington, D.C.

MUSICAL CONVERSATION

Baptist churches in the US are the original home of gospel music, in which the preacher and congregation create an emotional musical conversation. The excitement of gospel music, with its sliding melodies, joyful shouts, and other vocal effects, has had a huge influence on singers in many diverse areas of modern music, from soul to rock.

THE KING

Rock and roll legend Elvis Presley learned to sing in his local church choir, and was influenced by gospel music. He combined this with rhythm and blues and country music to create a unique style. Later in his career, he recorded unique versions of a number of hymns and carols.

GRACEFUL GOSPEL

Soul singer Aretha Franklin is the daughter of a preacher and a gospel singer from Detroit. She sang with her father's choir before starting to make her own records. Her music is powerfully emotional and full of strong vocal effects, showing her roots in gospel music. Her album *Amazing Grace* is a collection of reworked gospel songs.

Index

A

abbots, 30, 31, 44, 48, 54
Abraham, 7
Acts, Book of, 17, 18, 21
Advent, 56
All Souls Day, 57
altars, 50, 51, 52
angels, 8, 17, 26–27, 55, 60
Anglicanism, 35, 36, 48, 49, 52–53, 58
annunciation, 8, 32
Antioch, 19
Antony, St., 44
Aramaic, 20, 22
art, 60–61
ascension, 17
aspergillums, 17
assumption, 31
Athos, Mount, 33
Augustine, St., 41

B

baptism, 8, 10, 33, 50, 58
Baptist church, 58, 63
Becket, Thomas, St., 43
Benedictines, 44, 46, 48
Benediction, 28
Bernadette, St., 42
Bethlehem, 8, 56
Bible, 20–25, 32, 34, 36
 Gospels, 8–9, 11, 16, 17, 20, 21, 23, 52
 Latin, 24
 modern, 25
 New Testament, 17, 18, 20–21,
 Old Testament, 6–7, 20–23
 polyglots, 25
 texts, 22–25
 translations, 20, 34–35
bishops, 30, 31, 33, 36, 48
Book of Common Prayer, 35
Book of Hours, 55
Booth, William, 38
breviaries, 54
Brigid, St., 40
Byzantine empire, 19

C

Caiaphas, 15
Calvary, 15
Calvin, John, 34, 38
candles, 45
carols, 54, 63
cathedrals, 29, 32, 43, 61
Catholicism, 26, 28–31, 34, 40, 42, 44, 46, 48, 49
censers, 28, 29
chalices, 52–53
Chaucer, Geoffrey, 43
Christmas, 48, 54, 56, 63
churches, 36, 50–51
Compostela, 42, 43
confession, 28
confirmation, 33, 58
Constantine I, Emperor, 19
Constantinople, 19, 33
Coptic church, 44
Cranmer, Thomas, 35
creation, 6, 20, 54, 55
crèches, 56
Creed, Charles, 19
crosses, 16, 32, 54
croziers, 31, 33, 48
Cromwell, Thomas, 35
Crucifixion, 10, 14–15, 26, 56

D

Daniel, 7
David, King, 21
Dead Sea Scrolls, 22
desert fathers, 44
devils, 27
Deuteronomy, Book of, 22
disciples, 10, 12, 17, 18, 32
divine office, 45, 46

EF

Easter, 48, 56, 57
Eden, Garden of, 6
Emmaus, 17
Ephesus, 19
Epiphany, 56
Epistles, 18, 21
Erasmus, Desiderius, 35
Erasmus, St., 41
Essenes, 22
Eugenius IV, Pope, 29
Eustace, St., 42
evangelism, 39
festivals, 31, 56–57
films, 60, 62
Fox, George, 36
funerals, 58, 59

G

Gabriel, Angel, 8, 31
Galilee, Sea of, 10, 11
Genesis, Book of, 6, 7, 22, 27
George, St., 40
Gethsemane, Garden of, 15
God, 6, 7, 9, 12, 26, 54
Good Samaritan, 12
Greek, 20, 22, 23, 35
Gutenberg, Johannes, 24, 34

H

Hail Mary, 30, 31
Heaven, 6, 16, 26–27, 39
Hebrew, 6–7, 20, 22–23
Hell, 6, 26–27
Henry II, King, 43
Henry VIII, King, 35
Herod, King, 9, 20
Holy Communion, 14, 32, 47, 52–53
Holy Spirit, 8, 10, 18, 26, 33, 56, 58
Holy Trinity, 26, 41, 56
holy water, 29, 43, 50
honey, 47
Host, 28, 29, 47
Hubert, St., 41
Hus, Jan, 34

IJ

icons, 32
Ignatius, St., 49
incarnation, 8
incense, 28–29, 46
indulgences, 34, 35
Isaac, 7
Isaiah, 7
Jacob, 27
James, St., 42
Jeremiah, 21
Jerome, St., 24
Jerusalem, 14, 20, 57
Jesuits, 49
Jesus, 29, 60
 baptism, 8, 10, 58
 life, 8–10, 63
 death and resurrection, 10, 14–17
 teachings, 10–13
Jews, 6–7, 14, 20, 22-23, 54
Job, Book of, 21
John the Baptist, 8, 56, 58
Jonah, 21
Jordan River, 8
Joseph, 8, 9, 41
Joseph of Arimathea, 16
Judas Iscariot, 15
Justinian I, Emperor, 19

KL

Knights of St. John, 45
Lamb of God, 16
Last Judgment, 16, 26
Last Supper, 14, 15, 52
lecterns, 51
Lent, 56, 57
Lord's Prayer, 13, 30
Lourdes, 42
Lucy, St., 40
Luther, Martin, 34, 35
Lutheran church, 36

M

Madonna, see Mary
Magi, 9, 50, 56
Mardi Gras, 57
marriage, 58, 59
martyrs, 19, 40–41
Mary, 8, 9, 26, 30, 31, 32, 41, 58
Mary I, Queen, 35
Mary Magdalene, 10, 17
Mass, 28, 29, 30, 52
Maurice, St., 41
Mayflower, 36–37
Mennonites, 39
Messiah, 7, 15, 18, 56
Methodism, 36, 37
Michael, St., 6
Middle Ages, 25, 50, 54
millennium, 47
miracles, 10–11
missionaries, 19
miters, 30, 48
monasticism, 33, 35, 44–47, 62
monks, see monasticism
monstrance, 28
Moses, 7, 20, 62
music, 55, 59, 60, 62–63

NO

nativity, 8–9
Noah, 7
nuns, see monasticism
oaths, 60
original sin, 6, 31
Orthodox church, 32–33, 40, 44, 46, 48, 49

PQ

Palm Sunday, 57
parables, 12–13
Passion plays, 62
patriarchs, 32, 33
Paul, St., 18, 19, 21
penance, 28, 42
Pentecost, 18, 48, 56
Peter, St., 15, 18, 29, 55
Pharisees, 11
pilgrimage, 28, 42–43
Pilgrims, 37
Pio, St., 41
Pontius Pilate, 15, 16
Poor Clares, 45
popes, 28, 29, 30, 32, 34
prayer, 13, 28, 30, 45, 55, 60
preaching, 37, 38
Presbyterianism, 38
Presley, Elvis, 63
priests, 28, 30–32, 48–49
prophets, 7, 8, 14, 21
Protestantism, 34, 35, 36–39, 48
Proverbs, Book of, 21
Psalms, Book of, 21, 24, 41, 54, 62
pulpits, 51
Purgatory, 26
Puritans, 36, 37

Quakers, 36

R

Reformation, 24, 25, 34–35
relics, 42–43
Resurrection, 16–17, 26, 56
Revelation, Book of, 27
Roman Catholics, see Catholicism
Romans, 14, 18, 19, 22, 40
rosaries, 28, 30, 45

S

Sabbath, 54
sacraments, 49, 58
saints, 28, 30, 40–43, 61
Salvation Army, 38–39
Satan, 6, 27, 39
Saul, 19
second coming, 12, 26, 56
Sermon on the Mount, 12–13
sermons, 36, 51, 54
serpent, 6
Seventh Day Adventists, 39
Shakers, 36, 38
Sheba, Queen of, 20
shrines, 28, 42
Simon of Cyrene, 15
sin, 6, 8, 16, 26, 28, 42, 54
Solomon, King, 20
stained glass, 7, 10–11, 50, 61
Stephen, St., 19
stigmata, 41
synods, 33

TU

Ten Commandments, 20
Thomas, 17
Torah, 22–23
Trent, Council of, 24
Tyndale, William, 25
Urban VIII, Pope, 29

VWZ

Vatican, 29
vestments, 30, 33, 36, 48–49, 56
vicars, 49
Virgin, see Mary
Vulgate, 24
wafers, 47, 53
Wesley, John, 37
wise men, see Magi
Wyclif, John, 34
Zechariah, 14
Zwingli, Ulrich, 34, 39

Acknowledgments

Dorling Kindersley would like to thank models: Father Francis Baird, Father Stephen Horton, Julian Brand, Valerie Brand, Sister Susanna Mills, Sister M. Anthony, Sister Irene Joseph, Rev. Malcom Allen, Rev. Stephen Tyrrell, Rev. Felicity Walters, and Amber Mullins. **With special thanks to:** the monks of Prinknash Abbey, Cranham, UK, and the nuns of the Convent of Poor Clares, Woodchester, UK.
Index: Chris Burnstein.
Scripture taken from the HOLY BIBLE, NEW INTERNATIONAL VERSION®. NIV®. Copyright© 1973, 1978, 1984 by International Bible Society. Used by permission of Zondervan. All rights reserved.

The publishers would like to thank the following for their kind permission to reproduce their photographs: a=above; b=below; c=center; l=left; r=right; t=top

AKG London: 6br, 17tr, 19cb, 20bl, 21tl, 26tr, 33tl, 35tc, 36bc, 38tl, 38tc, 43t, 43t; British Library 63t; Erich Lessing 6tl, 7bc, 7cbr, 7r, 11bl, 15C, 18tr, 20tr; **alamy.com:** 28bc; Brian Harris 54b; **All Saints Church:** 2tl, 26br, 27tr, 27cl; **Ancient Art & Architecture Collection:** 10clb, 14r, 17tl, 61br; R. Sheridan 26tl, 27cr; **Arcaid:** Alex Bartel 32tl; **Bridgeman Art Library, London/New York:** 12cr, 21b, 25br, 35bc, 35br, 38c, 41clb, 41bcl, 61bl; Alte Pinakothek, Munich, Germany 41cla; American Museum, Bath, Avon 38cl; Bibilioteque Mazarine, Paris 21cr; Bible Society, London, UK 23tr, 23br; Biblioteca Publica Episcopal, Barcelona 49bc; Bradford Art Galleries and Museums 34bl; British Library, London, UK 24br; The Fine Art Society 38bl; Instituto da Biblioteca Nacional, Lisbon 21cl; Koninklijk Museum voor Schone Kunsten, Antwerp 49tr; Musee Conde, Chantilly, France 26cl; Museo di San Marco dell' Angelico, Florence, Italy 18bl; Museum of the City of New York, USA 37tl; National Museum of Ancient Art, Lisbon, Portugal 41c; Private Collection 27br; Rafael Valls Gallery, London, UK 36cal; Richardson and Kailas Icons, London 32cal; Six Parish Church, Haute-Savoie, France 30c; Victoria and Albert Museum, London 26bc; Wesley's Chapel, London, UK 37tr; **British Library:** 24tr, 24bl, 54c; **British Museum:** 1c, 16r, 22ca, 29tr, 29tr, 42c, 43br, 48tl, 59cr; **Corbis:** 61bl; Dallas and John Heaton 29br; Peter Turnley 63cr; Philip Gould 59br; **Danish National Museum:** 14t; **DK Picture Library:** Barnabas Kindersley 56tr, 56tr, 56tr, 56cl, 56br, 57bl; **Mary Evans Picture Library:** 12tr; **Florence Nightingale Museum:** 32bc; **Getty Images:** Allsport 60tl; **Sonia Halliday Photographs:** 10c, 16bc, 19cla, 21c; Laura Lushington 9br, 12cl; **Jewish Museum:** 22b, 23bl; **Museum of London:** 39ca, 39ca, 43cra; **Museum of Order of St John:** 45tr, 53bc, 54tl; **National Gallery, London:** 16bl, 17bl, 17br; **National Maritime Museum:** 17br; **National Museums of Scotland:** 43bl; **Christine Osborne:** 42tcl, 58bl; Liam White 47tr; **Panos Pictures:** Adrian Evans 36cl; Alain le Garsmeur 39cra; Jan Hammond 39c; Eric Miller 60br; Chris Sattlberger 37cr, 59tr; Paul Smith 39br; **The Picture Desk:** Art Archive Monastery of Santo Domingo de Silas, Spain/ Dagli Orti (A) 17ca, Diocesan Museum,Vienna/ Dagli Orti 31br; **Pictorial Press Ltd:** 62bl, 62br; **Powerstock Photolibrary:** 33tr; **Prinknash Abbey, Gloucestershire, UK:** 44cr, 50br, 51bl; Robin W. Symons 46c; **Zev Radovan, Jerusalem:** 10br, 20r, 22tl, 22c; **Royal Museum of Scotland:** 51tl; **Russian Orthodox Church, London:** 32c, 33c; **Saint Bride Printing Library:** 34c; **Scala Group S.p.A.:** 8bl, 10tl, 10tr, 14bl, 15br, 18br, 19tr, 20cl, 35tl, 42tl; Pierpont Morgan Library/Art Resource 10cl; **Science Museum:** 40c; **Sir John Soane's Museum:** 4cal, 50cbr; **South of England Rare Breeds Centre:** 7bl; **Tearfund:** Jim Loring 41br; **Topham Picturepoint:** 19bc, 60tr, 60c, 62t; Image Works 63bl; UPPA Ltd 63br; **Wallace Collection:** 28tl, 28l, 34cl, 40cl, 41t; **Warburg Institute:** 54t; **York Archaeological Trust:** 20tl.

Jacket picture credits: **British Museum:** spine; **Getty Images/ Anthony Boccaccio:** front r; **Glasgow Museum:** front tcl, back tcl; **Royal Museum of Scotland:** front tcr, back tcr